Who In Astrology Are You?

Written By A. M. Douthit

Dedications

This book is dedicated to my children, my husband, my mom, my grandma, and my best friends. Thank you for listening to me ramble endlessly about the stars and how they connect to life. Thank you for encouraging me to write this book and for supporting me every step of the way.

To my readers, thank you for opening these pages, allowing the stars to guide you on your own journey, and letting me be your teacher. It is because of you that my dreams are coming true, and I hope this book brings you closer to understanding this ancient art.

And most importantly, to my inner child, who knew the universe before I understood it and held its deepest mysteries close to her heart. This is for you, little one, for never letting go of your dream to write, for your love and passion for astrology, and for always believing you could make a difference in the world. You did it!

Table of Contents

Introduction

When I was growing up in the Midwest, you wouldn't have guessed it, but my life was often... unpredictable. I was primarily raised by my mother and am her only child. My mother, a single mom, worked persistently to protect me from the toxicity in our lives, and we were constantly moving to find a sense of stability, something we both longed for. As we moved from place to place, I saw firsthand the strength it took for my mom to shield me from harm and a dangerous lifestyle that came along with my biological father.

She is one tough chick! An Aries, of course. Having my mom was everything to me, as she was my soul provider. Her love and protection always made me feel safe, even as the world around us seemed to change at a moment's notice. She continues to do an excellent job of protecting me and making me feel loved, but even with that, I always felt like life was just a little too random, and I needed to know more about the world outside me.

As I grew older, I found comfort in something that was totally unexpected and that most around me found repulsive: Astrology. It all started when I was about 10 years old, around the time I began babysitting for the kids in my neighborhood, something I now realize I was probably too young to do, but hey, it was the '90s!

After earning a little money, I would ride my 10-speed bike down the road to the store to buy a teen magazine (probably Seventeen, J-14, or Cosmo Girl), one of the ones that included horoscopes. I would eagerly flip to the horoscope section in the back and search for my Leo sun sign.

When I was a kid, I honestly didn't know much about astrology, but in it I found a sense of clarity and a way to expect the unexpected in the world around me. It gave me a glimpse into the future where I was in a world that made sense of my experiences, helping guide me during moments of fear and loneliness. Through astrology, I found something to connect to, something that helped me understand myself in a world that often felt chaotic and extremely overwhelming.

Growing up, Astrology has become not just a tool to help me in life, but a part of who I am and how I connect with others. Trust me, I talk about it a lot, just ask my family and friends. It has helped me make sense of the things I have been through, the events that defined my life, identify opportunities I could have, and find my true path. I have always been searching for my contribution to this world and the part I might play that will bring me fulfillment. Writing this book allows me to share my knowledge with you. Something that I genuinely love doing.

Astrology has always pulled me in and tugged at my heartstrings. I love sharing what I know about Astrology with others because it has helped me discover things about myself that I couldn't believe were right there, plain as day, in my birth chart. It gave me awareness of which career path I should align with, how my strengths and weaknesses work together or against each other, and how I can make decisions that are true to who I am. Over the years, I've used astrology to predict things, both significant and minor events that have profoundly shaped my life.

What really captivates me the most about astrology is its multidimensionality. This isn't one of those systems where everyone's chart is the same if they share the same rising sign; instead, it's a complex, layered map that reflects the uniqueness of every individual. It shines a light on every aspect of your life. Astrology offers insights into things that extend far beyond what a general horoscope is. Astrology can help you gain a deeper understanding of yourself and those in your life. Once it really clicks for you, which I do not doubt that it will, you might fall in love with astrology like I have.

Astrology is more than just your average daily horoscope that is based on only your sun sign; it's a reflection of your unique energy that you bring into the world. In this book, I'm going to show you how astrology can be an everyday tool for self-discovery and empowerment. It's not about mysticism; it's about real-life guidance you can use. You don't have to be "Woo" for that! You must be open to symbolism and wisdom that has been around for thousands of years.

This book is not just a one-time read, but a tool and a guide for your personal growth and self-discovery, helping you get to know the real you. You are not going to open this book up and know it all on the first day, unless I am wrong, and if so, then that's very impressive. Usually, it takes some time, a little bit of patience, and a deep love to really understand Astrology. Use it to explore your birth chart, understand your strengths and challenges, and tap into the universal energies that influence your life.

In this book, you will discover how you connect to the wisdom of the stars and create deeper connections with yourself and the people around you. Trust me, you can never know everything about Astrology the first time you learn it, or even, especially, almost 3 decades later, after you start. I hope that you will walk away from these pages with a greater understanding of yourself and the world around you.

Real quick, though, before we begin, make sure that you locate your birth chart. This way, you can reference it as you go through the book, helping you make sense of who you are, your purpose in this world, and so many other layers you might have never guessed could be written in something as poetic as the stars.

If you don't know where to find your birth chart, I suggest using an online birth chart calculator. Some popular and reliable options include:

- **astro.com**

- **astro-seek.com**

- **cafeastrology.com**

For the sake of this book, I'll be using the Whole Sign house system, as it's often the easiest for beginners to learn astrology. While I do sometimes mix techniques in my own work, I'll explain more about that later in the book. For now, sticking to Whole Sign will make following along and understanding the concepts much smoother for you.

Much Love and Many, Many Blessings,

Ashley Marie Douthit

"Astrology is the poetry of Astronomy"- Steven Forrest

What Is Astrology?

When people hear the word "astrology," many instantly think of Astronomy or horoscopes in the back of a magazine, kind of like I did. Some even say, "Ew, I don't believe in that!" However, astrology is so much more than what people really know. It's an ancient system, and at its center lies a map of life laid out before you, to help you discover your destiny and all the answers you have been longing to know about yourself and your existence. Before we plunge into the details of how to read your own chart, let's start with the basics. What exactly is astrology?

The origins date back thousands of years to ancient Mesopotamia, where early civilizations and various cultures observed celestial patterns in the sky. These patterns guided everything from their planting seasons to crucial decisions in times of war. As time passed, astrology spread across Egypt, Greece, and Rome, eventually evolving into the systems we recognize today.

When I think about the relationship between astronomy and astrology, it helps me to use an analogy when explaining the difference to others, which may also be helpful to you. Astronomy is like studying an old tree by inspecting it from the roots on the ground all the way up to its branches and leaves, the physical form. Astrology, on the other hand, is more like walking through the forest and paying attention to how that one tree interacts with its surroundings, observing how it responds emotionally or metaphorically. This isn't just about the tree's structure, but also how it is connected within the larger forest, how it responds to the changing seasons, and how it interacts with other trees around it. While astronomy focuses on the technical and physical processes of the sky, astrology helps us understand the meaning of the stars and the story behind the cosmic movements.

All the way from Mesopotamia, astrology made its way to Egypt, Greece, and Rome, where it became more advanced and cultivated. You might have heard of Ptolemy, a famous Greek astronomer and astrologer (yes, he did both!). He wrote one of the earliest books about astrology called *Tetrabiblos*. Back then, astrology wasn't seen as separate from science or religion; it was all interlocked and didn't really split until the 17th & 18th centuries, when Astrology began to move from the scientific world into a spiritual realm.

Fast forward to the Middle Ages, and here astrology was flourishing in both the Islamic world and in Europe. It wasn't until the Enlightenment era, when science and rationalism gained prominence, that is when astrology began to lose credibility in the eyes of scholars. Despite that shift in perspective, astrology has remained well and thriving today, thank goddess! Now, it has evolved into a modern day map for self-discovery and personal growth today.

What I love the most about astrology is that it has stood the test of time. This is some ancient stuff! Even with all the changes in human history, people have continued to look to the stars for guidance and inspiration. People used astrology not just to determine how they loved or when they might marry, but also to help them with agriculture and find the best time to harvest; it was an integral part of their religious and spiritual practices. In ancient Babylon and Egypt, and later in Rome, astrology was used in royal courts, where court astrologers were employed to interpret omens and help ensure the court's success, as well as to ward off disasters. They would analyze the king's birth chart to determine how well they might rule. Needless to say, Astrology is and was important.

If I had to choose one phrase that captures my true connection to spirituality, it would be "as above, so below." This phrase, rooted in Hermetic philosophy, reflects the idea that there is a link between the universe and our lives. In simple terms, the movements of the planets and stars reflect what happens here on Earth and within us.

Now, this doesn't mean the planets control who you are. I'm not saying that Mercury or Neptune is up there pulling strings like some cosmic puppet master, even though sometimes, when they are in retrograde, things do tend to get a bit crazy. We do have this thing called free will, and because of this, we make our own choices; we aren't controlled. Instead, think of the planets as energetic markers. They reflect the cycles and themes we experience in our lives, which can manifest in various scenarios.

For example, take the Moon: its increasing illumination affects not just the night sky but also the ocean's tides through its gravitational pull. Humans are made up of about 60% water, so it makes sense that the

Moon's phases could influence our emotions. That's why many people feel more reflective or emotional during a Full Moon, especially depending on the Moon's sign. Astrology helps us understand and work with these natural patterns rather than trying to control them.

Now that we have covered some history, let's clear up some confusion: Are Astronomy and Astrology the same thing? The answer to this is a hard no. Astronomy is the scientific study of celestial objects, like the stars, the planets, and our galaxies. It's all about understanding the physical universe and what telescopes can see and scientists can find. On the other hand, astrology is the symbolic interpretation of how those celestial objects influence life on Earth and how they might influence you. Both are valuable, but they serve very different purposes. If you've ever gotten this confused with the other, no worries. This is a common misconception, and you are here to learn from it.

There are also several other misconceptions when it comes to Astrology, and I've heard a lot of them over the years of my exploring and learning the art of astrology. Here are a few that I've listened to:

"Astrology is just for entertainment purposes."

Sure, horoscopes can be fun, but astrology isn't just about predicting your day or finding out if you're compatible with your crush. Accurate astrology is a complex, multi-layered, and a highly personal subject. It's about understanding yourself, what your purpose is in this world, and all the cycles of life. It can be fun, exciting, informative, scary, and you could explore something from it for hours.

4

"Astrology isn't a scientific fact."

This question comes up often, and while it's true that astrology isn't a hard physical science, it doesn't need to be. Astrology is a symbolic system, more closely linked to psychology or philosophy than to physics. It offers insights and perspectives rather than definitive, measurable facts.

"Astrology says everything is predetermined."

Nope. Astrology is not about fate or fixed outcomes. It's about potential and possibilities. The things you may have experienced, but that isn't a certainty for everyone, with the exact placement. Your birth chart shows you the energies you're working with, but how you use those energies is up to you. Think of it like asking Alexa what the weather is like for the day, and it tells you it could rain. If that's the case, you may want to grab some rain boots and a jacket. Alexa is not a fortune teller and doesn't know exactly if that will happen. Sometimes that chick is wrong, but hey, getting a little heads-up never hurts anybody.

"I don't relate to my Sun sign, so astrology must not work."

Oh, this one is so common! I hear it ALL THE TIME! If you've ever read your Sun sign horoscope and thought, "This doesn't sound like me," don't worry, you're not alone. That's because your Sun sign is just one piece of the puzzle. Your full birth chart includes your Moon, rising sign, and all the planets, which together create a much fuller picture of who you are.

Fun fact: Try looking at your horoscope through the lens of your Ascendant (a.k.a. Rising sign). It will likely make more sense to you! You can even use all three (Sun, Moon, and Rising) for a more complete view! Astrology isn't about believing or not believing; it's about exploring. It's about being curious enough to ask, "What if there's more to my story?" because I bet there is.

Before we go any further, let me share something that really clicked for me when I was first learning astrology, and it might help you. I want you to think of a birth chart like a movie; every movie has its cast, plot, and setting. The **planets** are the characters in the film that bring energy into the story. The **signs** reveal **how** and **why** they explain the style of unfolding, the motivation behind it, and the personality those planets express outwardly. And the **houses** are the areas of your life where everything plays out.

Once I started seeing charts in this way, it stopped feeling completely overwhelming and began to make sense. Instead of staring at a wheel full of symbols that looked like pure French to me, I was able to read it as if it were a story about the soul's mission. That's the real magic in astrology: it doesn't just explain to you "who you are," but also shows you how the different parts of your life interact with others and how you evolve over time.

By the end of this book, you'll see how astrology can be practical, insightful, and even a little magical. For now, let's keep going. There is so much to unpack here, and if there is one thing that I am good at, it's talking about Astrology, and that, my new friend, takes some time. Get cozy, maybe grab a snack, and get ready to learn about the stars.

The 4 Elements

Let's call the corners, shall we? Just kidding. Let's talk about the four elements: Earth, Air, Fire, and Water. These elements shape the energy of different zodiac signs and represent them in unique ways. Earth includes Taurus, Virgo, and Capricorn. Air includes Gemini, Libra, and Aquarius. Fire rules Aries, Leo, and Sagittarius. Cancer, Scorpio, and Pisces represent the element of Water.

Breaking down each element will help you understand the collective spirit of what the signs represent and what that truly means. For example, Earth signs are going to be very practical and grounded. Often, the hard workers of the zodiac, the nurturing ones who create that home full of stability and structure. These individuals prioritize feeling safe in their environment and relationships, valuing consistency and long-term security above all else. They are the builders, the planners, and the ones who bring dreams into physical reality. These signs are managed by structure and family, rather than independence.

Air signs are different; they thrive more in the realms of ideas, communication, wit, and intellect. These are your social butterflies, free thinkers, and visionaries who seek knowledge and new perspectives. These individuals crave intense mental stimulation and often find themselves drawn to discussions, debates, and creative brainstorming. If they don't have that to look forward to, you can find them feeling bored. If they get

8

that way, they tend to get lost in their own head and thoughts. These signs are more guided by logic than by emotion.

Fire signs bring on the passion, high energy, and resilient enthusiasm wherever they go. These people are often very outgoing and can be seen as social butterflies, but in a more playful, get-out-and-have-fun type of way. They are the people who possess leadership-type qualities, the risk-takers willing to do anything for the sake of the plot at the most random times, and the ones who lead with confidence and charisma. Their spontaneity and boldness make them naturally attractive leaders who stand out in a crowd. These people are always ready to chase their desires with fierce determination, no matter the cost. Their passion and desire for freedom lead these signs.

Water signs are deeply intuitive people, often coming across to others as emotional, and they hold a strong connection to their spiritual side. They walk through life, deeply feeling their emotions and often absorbing the feelings of those around them. These are the empaths of the zodiac. These signs are the healers to others, the mystics and spiritual guides, and the ones who find meaning in insightful connections, their creativity, and their spirituality. These signs are accompanied by their emotional connections, seen or unseen, and express themselves creatively.

What are Modalities?

Astrology involves so much more than just the twelve zodiac signs and their elements. Another important layer of understanding astrology comes from knowing the three modalities, also known as qualities. Modalities describe how a sign expresses its energy and approaches challenges, and how each sign navigates life cycles. Each zodiac sign belongs to one of the three modalities: Cardinal, Fixed, or Mutable. These groups help explain the different and unique ways in which signs support and adapt to change. While the elements define a sign's natural core energy, the modalities decide its sequence and where it approaches life's cycles.

The Three Modalities

Cardinal Signs mark the start of each season, bringing fresh energy, motivation, and change.

Fixed Signs are the heart of each season, providing endurance and structure.

Mutable Signs ends each season. They adapt easily and transform to prepare for what's next.

Cardinal Signs: Aries, Cancer, Libra, Capricorn

Cardinal signs get things moving along; they are the zodiac's initiators, always eager to start something new. Each connects with the start of a season, bringing drive, ambition, and courage to take the first step.

Aries is a bold fire sign that marks the beginning of Spring. Aries faces challenges without hesitation, charging full speed ahead without overthinking it. This season marks the astrological New Year in March, a time for new beginnings.

Cancer is an emotionally sensitive water sign that has a naturally nurturing aura. This season marks the start of Summer, bringing warmth and long, sunlit days. Cancer energy is very nostalgic and loves spending time with loved ones. This energy encourages us to reflect on our family and summers past during this time, honoring the emotional connections and bonds that shape how we care for those around us.

Libra is a social and thoughtful air sign that brings in the beginning of Autumn. This is a season of balance and reflection, a time to truly look within. The bright, warm glow of summer has faded, and now we enter a world where everything begins to slow down to prepare for winter. Libra season is all about finding balance in our relationships with others and with ourselves. This is a time to release what no longer serves us while we are reminded that growth often comes from some of the hardest life lessons in learning to let go.

Capricorn is a strategic and disciplined earth sign that begins the winter season. This is a time for planning and perseverance as the world grows colder and slows down. This is perfect for conserving energy in the coming months. Capricorn energy loves structure, appreciates patience, and builds their long-term success by doing one thing at a time in a steady effort. This is an excellent time to work diligently towards achieving your goals and trust the process, even if it is progressing slowly.

Fixed Signs: Taurus, Leo, Scorpio, Aquarius

Fixed signs are the pillars of the zodiac, providing stability and structure within the astrological wheel. They build on what the cardinal signs started and help it develop into something beautiful through persistence and dedication. Each fixed sign relates to the middle of each season. This brings in that focus and determination to get things done!

Taurus is a grounded and sensual earth sign that excels in the heart of Spring. Taurus energy is patient and steady, with a deep appreciation for the physical world. This is a season of growth and abundance, as the earth awakens from its winter sleep, nature bursts into warmth and vibrance. This is a time to slow down and enjoy the rewards of our labor and the pleasures that surround us. This energy encourages us toward long-term stability and success.

Leo is a confident and radiant fire sign that shines its brightest at the height of Summer. Leo energy is warm, bold, and full of creative self-expression that naturally draws in the attention of others, only by using their enthusiasm for life and charm. This is a season of joy and vitality as we experience long summer days. Leo season encourages us to share our talents with others and to be playful.

Scorpio is an intense and determined water sign that comes in the middle of Autumn. Scorpio energy is deep and ever-changing, ready to explore the hidden layers of life. Scorpio season is a time of letting go and reflecting on the connection to death and rebirth. Scorpio energy encourages us to release what no longer serves us and to confront our shadows, the things that we don't really talk about or show to others.

Aquarius is a visionary and independent air sign that comes into focus during the center of Winter. Aquarius energy is inventive and loves to challenge social norms. They don't mind breaking tradition for something better to come along. Aquarius energy encourages us to embrace new ideas that come to mind and to think differently, not to march to the same drum as everyone else.

Mutable Signs: Gemini, Virgo, Sagittarius, Pisces

Mutable signs are the shapeshifters of the zodiac who are always ready to explore change and evolution. Mutable signs mark the last phase of each season, preparing for fresh beginnings. Their energy is adaptable, allowing them to see life from different perspectives and to help guide others through transition. Their influence highlights the importance of flexibility, learning, adapting, and the wisdom that can be gained from change.

Gemini is a quick-witted and talkative air sign that comes in at the end of Spring. Gemini energy is characterized by playfulness and liveliness, as they constantly explore new ideas and discover innovative ways to connect with the world around them. Gemini season is a time of mental stimulation and curiosity, a time when socializing with others takes center focus. Gemini energy encourages us to be open-minded and inquisitive while embracing change and learning from every experience.

Virgo is a thoughtful and detail-oriented Earth sign that arrives at the end of Summer. Virgo energy is hardworking, practical, down to earth, and dedicates its time to improving, not just themselves, but the world around them. Virgo season is a time to prepare and get organized as the carefree summer days start to fade away. Virgo energy inspires us to show up with mindfulness and purpose, encouraging us to bring order to our lives and support our long-term growth from within.

Sagittarius is an adventurous and free-spirited fire sign that marks its way at the end of Autumn. Sagittarius energy is optimistic, blunt, bold, curious, and explorative. Sagittarius season is a time to seek out new experiences, whether that be through traveling, learning, or just gaining fresh insight into other cultures. Sagittarius energy encourages all of us to embrace our freedom and expand our perspective.

Pisces is an intuitive and compassionate sign that arrives at the end of Winter. Pisces energy is dreamy, ethereal, empathetic, creative, and is strongly connected to the other side. Pisces season is a time to reflect and surrender in solitude as the world changes and prepares us for the rebirth

14

of Spring. Pisces energy encourages us to trust our intuition and embrace our imagination, while seeking meaning beyond the physical world.

The three modalities form the foundation of the zodiac's flow, each shaping its endless cycle of growth and evolution. Cardinal signs initiate the start of each season, bringing new energy and direction. Fixed signs anchor the middle, providing stability and focus. Mutable signs close each season, preparing the way for fresh beginnings.

The Zodiac Signs

The zodiac is a celestial wheel divided into twelve signs, each representing a unique human experience. These signs are energetic archetypes shaped by ruling planets, elements, and modalities, offering comprehension into our personality traits, life path, and place in the universe. Each sign brings distinct strengths and challenges.

Think of the zodiac as a cosmic clock, each sign marking a phase in life's cycle. Aries begins the journey, awakening new beginnings. Each of the following signs builds on the last, guiding us through stability, love, loss, self-expression, transformation, endings, and wisdom. This steady flow mirrors life's gradual changes, reminding us that growth is a process.

Beyond personality traits, the zodiac reveals our inner world and the external forces shaping us. Understanding the signs brings clarity about your purpose and helps you align with your true self. Whether you connect most with your Sun, Rising, or Moon sign, the zodiac outlines self-awareness and growth.

Astrology is so much more than you think, more than most comprehend.

Astrology isn't just about predicting the future and knowing who we are; it's about connection. It connects us to ourselves, to others, and to the vast cosmic energies that have guided humanity for centuries. The wisdom of the stars serves as a map unlike any other. No matter where you are on your path, the cosmos is always there, offering you guidance, insight, support, and a simple reminder that we are all part of something greater.

Aries

Cardinal · Fire · Mars · Head

March 21 - April 19

Let's begin with the baby of the Zodiac: Aries, the first spark of the astrological wheel. Aries personifies bold beginnings and is ruled by Mars, the planet of war and aggression. Aries is one of the zodiac's most energetic and determined signs, embodying competitiveness and assertiveness, and represents the House of Self.

Aries energy is characterized by enthusiasm; they are highly competitive and always want to be first or number one. People born under this sign have a distinctive drive to act and are rarely afraid of risks or challenges. Aries don't just dream about change in their life; they make it happen. They are most useful at starting new projects and bring the power to fuel that passion. This sign is perfect for starting any new projects or planting seeds of opportunity.

If you are an Aries or have your Sun, Moon, or Rising in Aries, you dislike waiting and prefer to act for yourself. Your energy is spontaneous, and you are always ready for action, showing natural leadership. You thrive on challenges, taking risks, and driving forward in life, always to keep going. Patience may not come easily, but your determination fuels your passion and intensity in all you do.

The ram symbolizes Aries' strong will and readiness to face challenges head-on. Aries are strong-minded, fearless, and natural leaders who inspire others with their drive and ambition. Their headstrong nature can lead to impulsiveness, causing them to enter situations without considering the consequences, but their courage often sees them through.

Aries is a Cardinal sign, marking the beginning of new seasons and new beginnings. Cardinal signs initiate change; a role Aries embraces. Physically, Aries rules the head, symbolizing forward-thinking and action. Those with Aries placements may lead with their head, sometimes experiencing headaches from pent-up energy. They thrive on challenge and toughen in adversity.

Astrologically, Aries marks the start of the year for many practitioners. Its season begins on March 21 and runs through April 19. Aligning with the Vernal Equinox, the official start of Spring. This is a time of renewal and regeneration, both in nature and within us. After the reflective haze and spiritual depth of the Pisces season, the Aries season feels like the first breath of fresh air. It's time to shed the past, plant new seeds, and embrace renewed confidence. This invigorating energy aligns perfectly with Aries' bold and daring personality, making it the spark that lights the astrological calendar.

Aries, the zodiac's first sign, traces back to ancient times. Approximately 2,500 years ago, the Babylonians divided the sky into 12 sections, each corresponding to a constellation. Aries, aligned with the spring equinox, symbolized beginnings and energy. In Greek mythology, the golden-fleeced ram sparked Jason and the Argonauts' quest, making Aries a symbol of boldness and new ventures.

Greek mythology deepened Aries' symbolism by sending the Golden Ram, sent by Zeus to rescue Phrixus (FRIK-suhs) and Helle (HEH-leh), making the ram a symbol of leadership and bravery. After the sacrifice, Zeus placed the ram among the stars as Aries. Babylonian astronomers and Greek myth together shaped Aries' courageous reputation.

During the Aries season, the days grow longer, and we start to feel the warmth of the sun returning. This is the time when we shake off winter's lethargy and rediscover our inner fire. The themes of this season include courage, independence, and embracing your own individuality. It's a time to take bold steps forward and let your ambition lead the way. The Aries season encourages us all to get out of our comfort zones and go after what we want with everything we've got. It's not a time to hold back. It's a time to act, to begin, and to believe in your ability to conquer whatever comes your way.

Famous Aries, such as Lady Gaga, Robert Downey Jr., Mariah Carey, and Maya Angelou, embody the fiery, adventurous spirit of this sign. Known for their fearless individuality and relentless drive, these icons inspire others to chase dreams.

Taurus

Fixed · Earth · Venus · Throat

April 20 – May 20

Taurus is the second sign of the zodiac, ruled by Venus, the planet of beauty, love, and pleasure. Represented by the Bull, Taurus is grounded, steady, and deeply connected to the material world. While Aries charges headfirst into action, Taurus teaches the value of patience, consistency, and enjoying life's simple pleasures.

If Taurus were a moment in life, it would be a long, leisurely afternoon spent in a beautiful garden, basking in the sunshine, savoring a delicious meal, or enjoying the comfort of a favorite cozy blanket, perhaps with music in the background. Taurus energy teaches us that it's okay to slow down and indulge in the good things life offers. This is the sign responsible for holding and maintaining momentum in both home and work environments.

At their best, Taurans are loyal, dependable, and patient. They're the friends you can count on to show up when you need them, offering both stability and warmth. They also have a deep appreciation for art, music, and anything that stimulates the senses. A Taurus will stop to smell the roses and maybe plant a garden while they're at it!

If you are a Taurus, or your Sun, Moon, or Rising sign is in Taurus, you likely value stability and possess a strong work ethic. Perhaps you are a bit stubborn, but it's simply that you know what you want and are not easily swayed. Your determination stands out, and once you focus on something, you see it through to the end. You probably have a deep appreciation for good food, cozy spaces, and anything that delights your senses. People might call you inflexible, but in truth, you crave security and consistency. Does this sound familiar?

But, as with all signs, Taurus has its shadow side. Their love for comfort and routine can sometimes translate into stubbornness or resistance to change. When a Taurus digs in their heels, it can be challenging to get them to budge. However, their persistence is also their superpower; once they commit to something, they'll see it through to the end, no matter what. These individuals can exhibit two distinct energy levels. They either prefer to relax and take it easy, or they dive headfirst into something with a bit of tenacious determination. Even a touch of ego, if I'm being honest.

Taurus, the bull, is the second sign of the zodiac, with origins dating back thousands of years. Evidence of its symbolism can be found in ancient cave paintings dating back to roughly 15,000 BC, which depict the bull as a powerful figure. The Babylonians associated Taurus with the "Bull of Heaven." In Greek mythology, Taurus is associated with Zeus, who transformed into a bull to carry off Europa. The bull has long symbolized strength, fertility, and abundance, traits that Taurus still embodies. Across cultures, the bull represents both power and the earth's nurturing aspects, reflecting Taurus as a sign grounded in life-sustaining energy.

In astrology, Taurus rules the second house, which governs resources, finances, and personal values. It's the sign that encourages building a solid foundation through financial security, a comfortable home, or meaningful relationships. Taurus teaches the importance of knowing our worth and living in accordance with our values. If you're a Taurus or have significant Taurus placements in your chart, you may feel most at peace surrounded by beauty, whether in nature or in a carefully curated space. You thrive when you feel safe and grounded, and when you're willing to work hard for the stability you desire.

Taurus invites us all to slow down, tune into our senses, and appreciate the richness of the world. Life isn't just about achieving goals; it's also about savoring the journey. This grounding energy is often drawn to nature and to values that naturally connect with the world.

Celebrity Taurans like Queen Elizabeth II, Adele, Sabrina Carpenter, David Beckham, and George Clooney embody the sign's dedication and success through perseverance. These individuals represent the reliable qualities that define Taurus, demonstrating their ability to achieve greatness through hard work and resilience.

Gemini

Mutable · Air · Mercury · Lungs & Nervous System

May 21 – June 20

Gemini, the third sign, is ruled by Mercury, the planet of intellect and communication. Represented by the Twins, Gemini shows duality, curiosity, and adaptability. Where Taurus is all about relaxation, Gemini brings excitement, connection, and possibilities. Socialization and mental stimulation define this sign.

If Geminis were a moment in life, they'd be you, chattin' it up with your BFF, jumping from topic to topic (maybe without taking a breath). That moment is filled with laughter, deep thoughts, and, let's be honest, probably some gossip. It could be the thrill of bouncing from social event to social event, or of discovering the latest gadget or book. Geminis remind us to keep things light and embrace connection. If you're a Gemini, or have placements in Gemini: Sun, Moon, Rising, you probably enjoy mental stimulation and crave variety in your approach to work, relationships, and tasks.

Geminis are quick thinkers and endlessly curious, thriving on new experiences and eagerly embracing change. They stand out as storytellers who effortlessly connect with others. Always ready for a challenge, they absorb information like a sponge and share insights widely. Geminis are natural idea makers and mediators, uniquely skilled at seeing multiple perspectives.

No sign is perfect; Gemini is no exception. Their love of variety can make them seem scatterbrained or non-committal. A bit of here, there, and everywhere, they might start many projects and finish only a few. Though adaptable, they can come across as flighty. Still, when a Gemini focuses on a passion, nothing can stop them. Their brilliance shines when they dig in deep.

The Twins symbol appears across ancient mythologies, including Greek mythology's Castor and Pollux. One is mortal, and the other is immortal, symbolizing Gemini's dual nature. This sign embodies the beauty of opposites and the connection that brings them into harmony.

In astrology, Gemini rules the third house, associated with communication, learning, siblings, neighbors, extended family, early education, and short-term travel. It's the sign that encourages us to ask questions, explore what's right in front of us, and make meaningful connections. Gemini inspires us to stay curious, adaptable, and open to new ideas and perspectives. Whether you're writing a book, teaching a class, or even just chatting with a stranger, Gemini reminds us of the importance of self-expression.

If you are a Gemini, or have your top three in Gemini: Sun, Moon, Rising, you feel most alive in stimulating conversations, exploring new ideas, and keeping your social calendar full. Sticking to one thing may be challenging, but multitasking is part of your magic. Wherever you go, you bring momentum and keep life interesting.

Gemini teaches us to embrace variety, curiosity, and learning as the main themes of life. Life is about discovering, not just mastering. Connected to the lungs and breath, Gemini also reminds us to stay grounded through open communication. Activities like journaling and honest conversation often help Geminis find peace and connection.

Celebrity Geminis, such as Marilyn Monroe, Kendrick Lamar, Johnny Depp, Stevie Nicks, and Morgan Freeman, exemplify the charisma and intellect of this sign. Gemini energy encourages you to be curious, communicate openly, and seek possibilities, just as these celebrities have.

Cancer

Cardinal · Water · Moon · Chest & Stomach

June 21 – July 22

Cancer is the fourth sign of the zodiac and a cardinal sign. Bringing us back to nurturing and emotion, Cancer is ruled by the Moon. Cancers are intuitive, protective, and attuned to the endless cycles of life. Represented by the Crab, they teach us the importance of emotional security and the value of a safe home for ourselves and our loved ones.

If Gemini burns brightly with mental energy turned outward, Cancer invites us to look inward, toward quiet reflection, heartfelt care, and the healing warmth of connection. Imagine sinking into the embrace of a loved one or savoring the comforting joy of a home-cooked meal. This is the soul of Cancer's caring energy. They pour tenderness into the spaces they create, ensuring everyone who enters feels cherished and at peace. Cancers take pride in making any place bloom with the spirit of home.

If you are a Cancer, or have your Sun, Moon, or Rising sign in Cancer, you may relate to nostalgia, deep emotions, and moments of retreat when faced with challenges. Going inward and finding a space alone helps you regain energy. Am I close?

At their best, Cancers are empathetic, loyal, and deeply caring. They intuitively sense what others need and offer support and comfort without judgment. Their homes are often sanctuaries filled with warmth, love, and a sense of nostalgia. Cancers are keepers of family traditions, ensuring everyone feels cared for, much like the comfort found in a batch of fresh cookies from a smiling grandmother.

Like every sign, Cancers face their shadows, too. Their remarkable emotional sensitivity can sometimes overwhelm them; like a crab, they may retreat into their shells at the slightest hurt, their moods shifting with the lunar cycle. Their love for the past can make old wounds slow to heal, but it is this same emotional depth that makes them resilient, guiding them with tenderness through even the most difficult times.

In Greek mythology, the Crab's story goes like this: Hercules had to slay the Lernaean, this fugly looking lake monster, Hydra. Hera, wife of Zeus, who hated Hercules, sent a crab to distract him. Hercules stomped it and continued fighting. Hera then honored the crab by placing it among the stars as Cancer. There's way more to that story, but you get the basics.

Cancer rules the chest and stomach, linking them to nurturing and emotions. They often feel emotions physically, so self-care is vital. For Cancer placements, self-care may mean taking alone time surrounded by comfort or having a good cry to process emotions. Taking "me time" is essential for their happiness.

Cancer governs the fourth house in astrology, which focuses on family, home, parents, and roots. This house highlights Cancer's love for creating stable, loving environments, whether through family ties or a cozy retreat.

Cancer season begins with summer, a time to deepen bonds and celebrate connections. It's a season to nurture ourselves and others, to embrace emotions, honor life's cycles, and reconnect with family and our roots.

Celebrity Cancers like Selena Gomez, Tom Hanks, Princess Diana, and Robin Williams embody emotional depth, creativity, warmth, intuition, and care. They remind us of the power of vulnerability and the strength that comes from connection.

Leo

Fixed · Fire · Sun · Heart & Spine

July 23 – August 22

Leo, the fifth sign of the zodiac, is ruled by the luminary Sun, the center of our solar system and a strong source of energy. Represented by the Lion, Leo embodies courage, confidence, and a charisma that shines brightly. Cancer teaches us about emotional security and nurturing, while Leo encourages us to express ourselves boldly and take center stage in our own lives.

If Leo were a moment in life, it would be the thrill of stepping onto a bright, lit-up stage, the warmth of heartfelt applause, or the joy of laughing in the sun with loved ones. Leo energy urges us to embrace our inner child, act independently, share our unique gifts, and lead with an open heart. Leos are natural leaders, always driven and energetic in achieving their goals. They love to embrace their creativity and are devoted to a fault.

At their finest, Leos are inventive, generous, fiercely loyal, and the life of the party. They naturally lead and ignite inspiration with their enthusiasm and vision. Leos flourish in settings where their talents can shine and make an impression, whether it's through the arts, leadership, or being the heart of every gathering. They are very outgoing and love being in a room full of their friends.

If you are a Leo, or have Leo as your Sun, Moon, or Rising sign, you probably enjoy attention, value independence, and dislike being micromanaged. You shine through your artistic talent and likely have a confident, fun-loving personality. You can succeed in environments that encourage self-expression and celebration. Skilled at entertaining, Leos hardly ever lack friends, and some with strong Leo placements even achieve fame. You have a youthful soul; you love being playful and creative. Sound like you?

Like every sign, Leo has challenges. Their desire for admiration can sometimes turn into attention-seeking or egotism. You could become a "Pick Me". Pride might make vulnerability difficult, and independence might make asking for help difficult. However, their courage and resilience help them overcome obstacles gracefully, and their natural warmth draws others in.

Leo's symbolism dates to ancient times. The sign is associated with Regulus (Latin for Little King), a star that stands out because the constellation looks like a lion. In Greek mythology, the constellation is linked to the myth of the Nemean Lion, a beast with a mysterious coat. It was almost impossible to hurt this lion.

The fur made it nearly impossible to penetrate with any weapon. Eventually, Hercules defeated the lion as part of his Twelve Labors and wore the coat. Many illustrations show Hercules wearing this prized possession. The lion represents strength, courage, and a royal presence.

Leos embody these qualities in daily life. Across cultures, the lion has always symbolized power and majesty. Leo carries this legacy forward.

In astrology, Leo rules the fifth house, governing creativity, self-expression, children, romance, and play. It is the house of joy and passion, letting us tap into what makes us feel most alive. Leo teaches us to honor life, awaken our inner child, and take pride in our creations.

Leo encourages us to kindle our inner light, to live genuinely, and lead with boldness and compassion. This reminds us that each person brings something unique to the table, and life deserves celebration. Such reminders highlight that each of us has a distinct gift to share with the world.

Famous Leos like Madonna, Jennifer Lopez, Barack Obama, and Daniel Radcliffe exemplify the sign's magnetic presence, creativity, and leadership. They demonstrate the power of embracing uniqueness and living courageously.

Virgo

Mutable · Earth · Mercury · Digestive & Nervous System

August 23 – September 22

Virgo, the sixth sign of the zodiac, is ruled by Mercury, the planet associated with the mind, intellect, communication, and detail. Represented by the female Virgin (or Maiden), Virgo embodies purity, precision, perfectionism, and a dedication to service. While Leo energy draws attention with grand gestures and bold self-expression, Virgo gently emphasizes the importance of attending to details and approaching tasks with care and intention.

If Virgo were a moment in life, it would be the satisfaction of completing a perfectly organized closet, from color-coordinated clothes to neatly arranged shoes. It is the pride in crafting a well-thought-out plan and watching it unfold as intended. There is relief in checking off another task from your to-do list, easing any anxiety. Virgo energy invites improvement, promoting discipline and an appreciation for the small efforts that enhance our daily lives.

At their best, Virgos are analytical, practical, hard-working, and deeply caring. They have a unique ability to see what needs to be done and how to do it effectively. As the healers of the zodiac, Virgos are often the ones quietly working behind the scenes, making sure everything runs smoothly.

33

This natural problem-solving ability helps them strive for excellence in every aspect of their lives, whether it's at work, at home, in relationships, or in pursuing personal goals. Because of this, Virgos can solve problems very efficiently, thanks to their ability to analyze any given situation.

Suppose you are a Virgo, or have Virgo placements such as the Sun, Moon, or Rising. In that case, you may be someone who enjoys improving situations for others, values organization, and feels compelled to keep things in order, often without asking others for help. You might carry some anxiety from taking on many responsibilities, often in an effort to maintain harmony. You could also have a perfectionist streak or focus on health-conscious habits. Does this resonate with you?

However, Virgo's pursuit of perfection can sometimes be their biggest downfall. Their strengths may also lead them to be overly critical of themselves or others, as they may tend to set impossible standards for themselves and others. This meticulous nature can lead to overthinking or to focusing on imperfections rather than the bigger picture. Still, their dedication and desire to serve or be of "help" often outweigh their inner struggles, ultimately making them one of the most reliable and resourceful signs.

The Virgin, symbolized by the constellation Virgo, is deeply rooted in ancient mythology and associated with goddesses Demeter, the Greek goddess of the harvest, and Astraea, the goddess of justice and purity. These figures embody themes of nurturing, balance, and the cycles of nature, reflecting Virgo's fundamental connection to service, health, and bringing structure to the world. Additionally, in Babylonian astrology, the constellation Virgo was known as "The Furrow" and symbolized the goddess of the harvest, often shown holding a bundle of grain to represent the fruits of the earth. Astraea's association with justice, loyalty, and duty further enhances Virgo's reputation as a sign devoted to integrity and order. Altogether, these connections highlight Virgo's reflective desire to work with the physical world, bringing diligence and precision to everything they touch.

In astrology, Virgo rules the sixth house, which governs daily routines, work ethic, pets, relationships with food, health, and service to others. This house naturally connects to the earlier themes of Virgo and teaches us the value of discipline, wellness, and creating a life of meaning through small, consistent acts.

If you are a Virgo or have significant Virgo placements (as I do with Virgo rising), you may feel most comfortable in orderly environments where you know what to expect. You likely thrive in settings where organization, analysis, hard work, health, and service are valued. You are constantly seeking ways to better yourself and your environment, continually striving for improvement.

Famous Virgos like Keanu Reeves, Zendaya, Mary Shelly, Steven King, and Freddie Mercury embody the sign's dedication, talent, hard work, and modesty. Their success serves as a reminder of the value of precision and staying true to our purpose, tying back to all the earlier qualities discussed throughout this reflection on Virgo.

Libra

Cardinal · Air · Venus · Kidneys, Lower Back, & Skin

September 23 – October 22

Libra, the seventh sign of the zodiac, is ruled by Venus, the planet of love, joy, beauty, and harmony. Represented by the Scales, Libra seeks balance in their life. They want fairness and connection. Where Virgo focuses on all details down to the pinpoint of accuracy, Libra's energy reminds us of the importance of close relationships, visual aesthetics, and the art of beauty and compromise. Libra is the peacemaker, striving to bring harmony to chaos and a little bit of love to the mix.

If you are a Libra, or have Sun, Moon, or Rising placements in Libra, you likely seek a peaceful life surrounded by the finer things, an equal balance of love and beauty. You value fairness for all and attempt to ensure everyone is treated equally. Enjoyment comes from good movies, good food, and pleasure (in various forms).

If Libra were a moment in life, it would be the sensation of entering a beautifully decorated room where every detail, from colors to textures, contributes to a sense of calm and connection. It is the excitement of hosting a party or gathering where everyone feels valued and enjoys themselves, or even the satisfaction of resolving a disagreement in a way that leaves all parties feeling seen and heard. Libra energy encourages prioritizing collaboration with others, finding beauty in surroundings, and seeking out fairness in all interactions.

At their best, Libras are charming, fair-minded people who are cautious and genuinely empathetic. They naturally bring people together and create harmony, making others feel welcome. Libras excel in negotiation, creativity, and collaboration, with a unique ability to see the perception from all sides. As hopeless romantics, they love to love and value meaningful connections, often holding relationships together, whether it's in family or friend circles.

Libra's desire for balance can lead to indecision, making it hard to choose what they want and sometimes leading them to procrastinate. Their aim for harmony can lead to conflict avoidance, even when it is needed. Libras may people-please and overlook their own needs for peace. At times, they focus on appearances or depend on validation from others, especially through words of affirmation. That is definitely their love language, along with physical touch. Still, their commitment to fairness often helps them overcome these struggles and shine as a supportive presence. Their drive for fairness for all can make it hard to trust their judgment, as they seek both peace and approval. Understanding this duality, we look to the symbolism that further enriches the Libra story.

The Scales, Libra's symbol, are rooted in ancient mythology. Early Arabic astronomers linked Libra's constellation to Scorpio, while other civilizations associated it with Virgo. Virgo was often depicted as Astraea, goddess of justice, holding the scales, which became Libra's trademark.

Libra is the only zodiac sign represented by an object. Eventually, Libra's Scales became a distinct constellation and zodiac sign.

This symbolism aligns perfectly with the Autumn Equinox, which occurs when the Sun is in Libra. During this time, day and night are of equal length, representing the essence of balance.

In astrology, Libra rules the seventh house, which governs relationships, one-on-one partnerships, and competitors, as well as connections. This house teaches the value of collaboration and mutual support, reminding us that life is better with strong bonds and that there are always two sides to a story. This relational energy becomes especially apparent in the lives of those with strong Libra placements.

Those with Libra or significant Libra placements often thrive in environments where beauty, balance, and relationships are the central language. Harmony, whether that's through meaningful connections or well-designed surroundings, brings a sense of fulfillment. The ability to see multiple viewpoints makes them excellent mediators, and their creativity often leaves a lasting impression.

Famous Libras like Will Smith, Confucius, Serena Williams, Gwen Stefani, and Mahatma Gandhi embody the sign's charm, creativity, and dedication to connection and justice. Their success highlights the Libra spirit of creating beauty, building bonds, and standing for what's fair and unbiased.

Scorpio

Fixed · Water · Pluto & Mars · Reproductive System & Bladder

October 23 – November 21

Scorpio, the eighth sign of the zodiac, is ruled by Pluto, the planet of renovation, and Mars, the planet of action and passion. In Traditional astrology, Mars was the sole planet associated with Scorpio. After Pluto's discovery in 1930, modern astrology adopted Pluto as its main planet ruler, with Mars being its sidekick. Represented by the Scorpion, Scorpio exemplifies intensity, depth, and resilience. Where Libra seeks harmony, Scorpio plunges beneath the surface to uncover hidden truths, focusing on evolution.

If Scorpio were a moment, it would be finally confronting your deepest fears and releasing secrets to those closest to you, that even you kept hidden from yourself. This kind of truth, once revealed, can be shocking and a bit intense. So, buckle up, buttercup! It's the powerful feeling that comes after you rise from the ashes, stronger than you were before. Scorpio energy is about the continuous evolution of life and death, and the reflective transformation that takes place after.

If you are a Scorpio or have strong Scorpio placements, Sun, Moon, or Rising, you might be drawn to the darker side of life. Someone who keeps many secrets, may appear mysterious and intuitive, and may enjoy some mysticism on the side. These individuals often need to retreat when they are emotionally overwhelmed and seek peace in solitude. From my experience with my Scorpio-filled family, they also crave space after too much social interaction.

At their best, Scorpios are intensely passionate, imaginative, committed, and extremely faithful. They face life's shadows fearlessly, which makes them intuitive and resilient. When seeking answers, they pursue them with intense determination. Scorpios excel in roles that demand emotional depth, investigative skills, or groundbreaking leadership; they aren't fond of being told what to do. They observe others carefully, waiting for the right moment to act. They always find things out and use their insights for growth and healing, making them strong leaders, analysts, or private detectives. A true Scorpio never takes things at face value.

On the other hand, do you ever notice that Scorpios' intensity can lead to secrecy or a need for control? Do they sometimes come off as a bit shady? Sorry, that was just a joke for my Scorpio part of my family, but all jokes aside, maybe you recognize your own powerful emotions, like jealousy or a fear of revealing your feelings to the wrong person. Still, your courage and drive for change often result in impressive personal growth. Scorpio energy is full of sexuality and passion; you might even find excitement in the art of seduction and taboo topics. Do these traits resonate with you? I bet they do, you naughty little thing.

The Scorpion, Scorpio's symbol, and Scorpius, the constellation, are linked to themes of death and rebirth. Representing the life-changing power of this sign. In ancient mythology, Scorpio is associated with the story of Orion and Artemis, where the Scorpion's sting brings finality. Another version involves Orion, who claimed he could hunt any animal. This angered Gaia, the goddess of Earth, prompting her to send a vengeful Scorpion to challenge Orion. After stinging Orion, both became constellations.

In astrology, Scorpio rules the eighth house: transformation, shared resources, taboo subjects, intimacy, the occult, inheritance, and life's mysteries, especially the ones about what happens when we die. Many Scorpios excel at communicating with the unseen and exploring the other realms. This house reminds us of growth through deep trust and connection. If you resonate with Scorpio, you likely flourish when circumstances demand depth and strength.

Famous Scorpios like Leonardo DiCaprio, Julia Roberts, RuPaul, SZA, Winona Ryder, Marie Antoinette, Ryan Gosling, and Pablo Picasso exemplify the sign's power, intensity, and transmutative energy. These passionate, successful icons possess an intuitive drive that has compelled them to take bold risks.

Sagittarius

Mutable · Fire · Jupiter · Hips, Thighs, & Liver

November 22 – December 21

Sagittarius, the ninth zodiac sign ruled by Jupiter, personifies adventure and the pursuit of higher truths. While Scorpio is inwardly focused on evolving, Sagittarius looks outward. Eager for meaning through experience and exploration, even if it requires venturing out far and wide. This is the philosopher, the traveler, the wise one.

If Sagittarius were a life moment, it would be a spontaneous road trip to some random place with your best friend for the sake of just getting out of town and letting your hair down. It's the thrill of broadening your learning and the freedom to chase your dreams without the fear of failure. Sagittarius energy embraces life with wonder, positivity, and a constant hunger for growth and knowledge.

Reflecting those qualities, at their best, Sagittarians are adventurous, kind, blunt, philosophical, giving, and free-spirited. They shine in roles that involve teaching, traveling, or inspiring others through their wide perception. Sagittarians are the natural optimists and cheerleaders of the zodiac who encourage others to see the bigger picture and live life to the fullest. If you want to surround yourself with someone who is full of life, encourages you to live your dream, and who goes on random adventures to who knows where, find yourself a Sagittarian.

Still, a Sagittarius's love for freedom can sometimes make them impatient or inconsistent. They may struggle with commitment, whether in relationships or their gym membership. Some avoid responsibility to maintain independence. Their blunt honesty, while refreshing to others, can sometimes seem thoughtless or unkind. Sags tend to spread themselves thin trying to accomplish all their big plans. Despite these trials and tribulations, their optimism and passion help them bounce back and inspire others.

The Archer is the Sagittarius's symbol, representing aiming for higher dreams and possibilities. In mythology, it's associated with the centaur Chiron. Chiron is a wise teacher and healer who shares knowledge and inspires us to grow despite our wounds. This underlines Sagittarius's connection to learning, exploring, adventure, and seeking meaning.

Another interpretation links the centaur symbol to Krotos, the son of Pan. Krotos is known for his exceptional archery skills and is credited with inventing archery in legend. Regardless of the mythological source, both of these figures feature the outgoing and meaning-seeking nature of Sagittarius.

In astrology, Sagittarius rules the ninth house, governing travel, philosophy, higher education, publishing, purpose, wishes, and spiritual growth. This house urges us to expand through new experiences, reflecting

Sagittarius's embrace of cultural differences and love of learning about the world.

In line with these themes, if you're a Sagittarius, Sag rising, or a lot of your planets are in Sagittarius, you probably thrive in environments that encourage freedom and adventure. You have a natural curiosity that draws you to explore the world or those bucket-list destinations you've always dreamed of visiting. Learning comes naturally to you, and even more so, you love sharing what you've discovered with others. This is where the natural teacher comes in.

Ultimately, there's a special kind of joy you experience when you're free to chase your dreams and witness the spark of understanding light up in someone's eyes as you teach or inspire them. That moment when the light bulb comes on. Sagittarius invites us all to embrace the power of curiosity and optimism. It's a reminder that life is a journey and every experience, good or bad, is an opportunity to grow and learn.

Famous Sagittarians like Taylor Swift, Tina Turner, Britney Spears, Sammy Davis Jr., Walt Disney, and Billie Eilish show adventure, creativity, and freedom. Their lives encourage us to dream big, live boldly, and cheer others on.

Capricorn

Cardinal · Earth · Saturn · Knees, Joints, & Skeletal System

December 22 – January 19

Capricorn is the tenth sign of the zodiac, ruled by Saturn, the planet of discipline, structure, long-term goals, and responsibility. Represented by the Sea Goat, Capricorn embodies ambition, persistence, and practicality. Sagittarius inspires us to have big dreams and go for them, while Capricorn ensures we make plans and persevere with our energy to make those dreams a reality, allowing us to slow down and be patient.

If Capricorn were a moment in life, it would be the happiness of achieving a long-term goal after years of consistent effort and determination. It is the fulfillment that comes from overcoming challenges and that sense of "I made it" at the end. Capricorn energy, and the season it represents, emphasizes the importance of stamina, tenacity, and a diligent approach in achieving success. This is a period for productivity, getting it done, and leaving no room for procrastination. It's time to make plans for building our future.

Suppose you are a Capricorn, or have prominent Capricorn placements such as the Sun, Moon, or Rising. In that case, you likely value achievement, tend to learn toward perfectionism, and consider a solid life foundation essential to living; you have to be cozy and comfortable.

At their best, Capricorns are disciplined, ruthless, accountable, and resourceful leaders. They do great in roles that demand organization, top-tier management, and planning, often delivering results aligned with their vision. Their inner strength ensures persistence, turning dreams into reality through discipline and perseverance.

Yet Capricorns' focus on success can sometimes make them overly critical or a bit workaholic. They may struggle to relax; they may not know how, or they could feel guilty about taking time off from work to put themselves first. Their high standards, both for themselves and others, can sometimes lead to feelings of defeat and feeling drained. Regardless, Capricorns' strength and determination often lead to great success in their lives.

The Sea Goat, Capricorn's symbol, vividly represents the capacity to conquer hardship through the mixing of dual forces. In mythology, this unique creature, a fusion of goat and fish, stands for the chemistry between material ambition (goat) and spiritual depth (fish). For Capricorns, this duality means striving for success and recognition in the physical world while remaining deeply attuned to inner wisdom and intuition. This blending of practical energy and spiritual aspiration focuses on Capricorn's ability to transform aloof ideals into tangible results.

In ancient times, the Babylonians saw the constellation Capricornus as the figure Capricorn. They imagined it as the Suhurmashu (Soo-hoor-mah-shoo), a magical creature with the front half of a goat and the tail of a fish, symbolizing Capricorn's dual nature. They might have linked it to Enki, the Sumerian god of wisdom, water, and creation, highlighting Capricorn's special ability to blend earthly knowledge with mysterious visions. The goat's strength and durability, along with the fish's flexibility, remind us of how success involves balancing achievements with inner wisdom. This idea that success isn't just about discipline, but also about mastering both material and emotional challenges, is quite inspiring. As Babylonian star stories traveled, they influenced Greek mythology, where Capricorn is associated with Pan, who had the legs and horns of a goat and was clever enough to leap into the water and transform: his upper half stayed a goat, while his lower half turned into a fish, helping him escape. To celebrate Pan's cleverness and adaptability, Zeus placed him among the stars as Capricornus, making this story a symbol of resourcefulness and resilience.

In astrology, Capricorn rules the tenth house, governing our career, public image, authority, and our long-term goals. This house asks us to consider our legacy and our impact on the world.

Famous Capricorns: Michelle Obama, Dolly Parton, Timothée Chalamet, Rob Zombie, Martin Luther King Jr., Kate Middleton, embody ambition, discipline, and grace under pressure. Their achievements show the value of their unwavering dedication.

Aquarius

Fixed · Air · Uranus & Saturn · Circulatory System &

Ankles

January 20 – February 18

Aquarius is the eleventh sign of the zodiac, ruled by rebellious Uranus. It was previously associated with Saturn, the planet of discipline and structure, until Uranus's discovery in 1781. Aquarius, represented by the Water Bearer, symbolizes progress, individuality, and originality. While Capricorn focuses on tradition, Aquarius looks into the future, embracing uniqueness and forward-thinking.

If Aquarius were a moment in life, it would symbolize the characteristics of joining a social movement to create a meaningful change in the world or collaborating with like-minded thinkers on advanced ideas. It is the fulfillment found in standing out from the crowd, thriving in independence, and accepting one's true self for who they are. Aquarius energy thrives on invention, community, and free-thinking solutions. Aquarians are natural helpers and humanitarians, always rooting for the underdog and motivated to make the world a better place. They are confident in their ability to contribute. They tend to resist authority, preferring sovereignty and avoiding constraints at all costs.

At their best, Aquarians are visionary, very independent, highly intellectual, and humanitarian to the core. They excel in roles that involve innovation, technology, or social change. Aquarians are natural leaders and thinkers who inspire others with their unique perspective and desire to make things better than they were found. Their dreams can help the whole world dream big. Freedom is the most important thing to them, and they want others to achieve it, too.

Nonetheless, Aquarius's focus on individuality and the desire for independent thinking, or simply a need for distance from others, can sometimes create an impression of detachment or as if they are avoiding you. Aquarians might experience challenges with emotional expression or feel misunderstood as they challenge conventional standards; they don't like normalcy. Their rebelliousness, while inspiring, can occasionally hinder collaboration with others. Despite these obstacles, Aquarius's originality and determination consistently promote meaningful progress and future change.

In mythology, the Water Bearer is associated with figures such as Ganymede, a prince of Troy who brought nectar to the gods, symbolizing Aquarius as a bringer of wisdom. Egyptians believed floods occurred when the Water Bearer tipped his jug, and Mesopotamians also linked Aquarius to floods.

In astrology, Aquarius rules the eleventh house, which governs friendships, social groups, and collective goals. This house encourages us to consider our role in the community. Though Aquarius is called the "alien" of the zodiac, it is only because they often feel they don't fit in, even as they strive to improve the world.

If you are an Aquarius or have significant Aquarius placements, you likely thrive in environments that value vision, innovation, creativity, and individuality. You may feel most engaged when challenging established norms, discovering novel approaches, or advocating for your beliefs. You recognize the multitude of opportunities available and the diverse avenues to achieve them.

Aquarius season encourages embracing technology, innovation, and community involvement. It serves as a reminder that progress arises from challenging norms and collaborating for a better future. This period encourages stepping out of comfort zones, sharing ideas, and questioning restrictive societal expectations.

Famous Aquarians like Oprah Winfrey, James Dean, Harry Styles, Jennifer Garner, Shakira, Bob Marley, and Galileo embody creativity, vision, and the humanitarian spirit. Their success urges us to think big and embrace our uniqueness.

Pisces

Mutable · Water · Neptune & Jupiter · Feet & Lymphatic System

February 19 – March 20

Pisces is the final sign of the zodiac. The twelfth sign ruled by Neptune, the planet of dreams, illusion, intuition, and imagination, in modern astrology. In traditional astrology, Jupiter, the planet of wisdom, prosperity, and expansion, primarily ruled Pisces. That is, until Neptune was discovered. Now, both planets co-rule this dreamy sign. With that foundation, let's look at the essence of Pisces and what truly defines this sign.

Represented by the Fish, Pisces stand for compassion, creativity, and an ethereal connection to the spiritual world. While Aquarius focuses on progress and thinking outside the box, Pisces dives (pun intended) into the depths of emotion and universal connection. Pisces enjoys good company and conversation and is very friendly, but tires easily and needs to learn what healthy boundaries are. This is something that many Pisceans often struggle with: the beautiful art of the word "no". Understanding these challenges adds nuance to the unique way Pisces experience life.

If Pisces were a moment in life, it would be the artist getting lost in a beautiful piece at a museum, or the comfort of granting yourself the opportunity to let out a heartfelt cry in the privacy of your dreamy bedroom. It's the attraction of feeling connected to something more powerful and greater than yourself. Pisces energy thrives in imagination, empathy, and spirituality. This is where it feels the most at home. Because of this, Pisces is often seen as the hippie of the zodiac: the artist, the psychic, the sensitive intuitive.

If you are a Pisces or have prominent Pisces placements, Sun, Moon, or Rising, you are likely in tune with your intuition and let it guide you daily. You may be spiritual, artistic, dreamy, compassionate, creative, poetic, and deeply, deeply emotional. When overwhelmed or emotionally spent, you may feel the need to retreat, as Scorpios and Cancers do. These tendencies underline how Pisces' deep emotional reservoir influences their everyday choices.

At their best, Pisceans are compassionate, artistic, intuitive, and selfless. They shine in unsurprisingly creative avenues, places of healing, or emotionally connected roles. Natural dreamers, they inspire others with their ability to find beauty and connect with the unseen. Pisceans are known for their talents in the spiritual and mystical realms. However, these same qualities can lead to certain difficulties.

Pisces's sensitivity can make them prone to escapism or gullibility. They struggle to set restrictions, often absorbing others' emotions as their own, feeling confusion about the blurred lines of whose feelings are whose, and needing solitude to recharge. Their dreamy nature, while inspiring, can lead to a loss of focus on practical realities, leaving them to go with the flow. Despite challenges, Pisces's empathy and creativity nurture beauty and healing. This delicate balance between strength and weakness is mirrored in Pisces' symbolic mythology.

The Fish, symbolizing Pisces, represents duality and the flow between physical and spiritual realms. Mythologically linked to Aphrodite, the goddess of love and beauty, and Eros, the God of love, who became a fish to escape Typhon, the weird-looking son of Gaia, the story tells us how the pair tied themselves together and leapt into the Euphrates River. Fish swimming in different directions emulating Pisces' tendency to be pulled in various ways and to be torn between goals. This opposition can lead to distraction, yet Pisceans are intuitive and know which way to go.

Pisces rules the twelfth house, governing spirituality, intuition, dreams, the subconscious, and endings, prompting reflection, release, and the embrace of mystery. If you have strong Pisces placements, you likely thrive in environments that promote creativity, dreams, and soul-level connection, feeling fulfilled when you express your creativity or help others heal. This connection to the unseen also emphasizes the imaginative and empathetic energy Pisces brings to the world.

Famous Pisceans like Rihanna, Albert Einstein, Chelsea Handler, Steve Jobs, Jensen Ackles, Elizabeth Taylor, and Kurt Cobain exemplify creativity, sensitivity, and vision. Their talents have made a mark on the world, each in their own unique way, by turning their dreams into reality, with success reflecting intuition, artistry, and a boundless vision.

The Planets

Our planets in astrology are like storytellers. Each one plays its own part in shaping our lives, actions, and growth. Zodiac signs show how we express energy, while planets show what parts of life are affected. The inner planets (Sun, Moon, Mercury, Venus, and Mars) influence our daily lives, while the outer planets (Jupiter, Saturn, Uranus, Neptune, and Pluto) affect broader life themes and spiritual development, but much more slowly.

Sun ☉

He is radiant, vibrant, and full of life. The Sun is the fire illuminating our world, shining its golden light on all that surrounds us. He is an inspiration, a guiding light, motivating our core and uncovering our inner wisdom. The Sun burns with steady strength, directing us toward our purpose and showing the path ahead. He allows us to see ourselves as we truly are and as we are meant to be. More than a source of warmth, he is the father or father figure, a masculine energy in astrology. Like an encouraging Father who wants the best for you, the Sun inspires resilience and growth, empowering us to shine as our most authentic selves.

The Sun is the center of our solar system, not a planet but a luminary influencing the changing seasons. In astrology, the Sun represents our life force, our core identity, and our conscious mind. It shapes our willpower and personal expression, and governs the ego, guiding how we see ourselves and how we want to be seen.

The Sun rules Leo, a sign known for its boldness and confidence. Just as the Sun is central to the solar system, Leo seeks the spotlight and thrives when being the center of attention. The Sun's energy is brave and radiant, promoting authenticity. A strong Sun in a chart implies a person with natural leadership and purpose, while challenges may lead to struggles with ego or self-worth.

The Sun spends 30 to 31 days in each sign, completing a 12-sign cycle every 365 days. When it returns to its birth position, it marks your Solar Return, a key astrological event shaping your year ahead. Your Solar Return, your Birthday, reveals personal themes, opportunities, and challenges you might experience in the year to come. Knowing this can help you become more self-aware.

The position of the Sun in your birth chart can reveal areas where you naturally excel and where your strengths are most noticeable. The zodiac sign it occupies describes how you express your individuality, while its placement in a specific house highlights the life area where your core identity is most active. This placement also points to qualities you develop over time and how you direct your energy outward. Understanding the Sun's position in your chart gives you perspective on your life purpose.

For example, if your Sun is in the first house, you take on Aries-like energy regardless of your zodiac sign. This placement is associated with a strong personal presence and expressive nature, often enjoying attention from others and recognition. While it can sometimes lead to a focus on self over other people, it also reflects an inherent drive to live authentically and be only who you were meant to be.

If you have your Sun in the 3rd house, you personify Gemini-like energy at your core. You have a deep connection to communication and how you process and share information. This placement often makes you naturally curious and an active participant in full-blown conversations. You are eager to explore new ideas and navigate discussions. You likely feel a strong need to connect with others, especially siblings, extended family, and neighbors. These relationships are integral to your sense of self. While you may excel at initiating and maintaining dialogues, you can sometimes be more talkative than attentive. This may make it challenging to listen while you speak.

The Sun is linked to Sunday, making it a powerful day for creativity, self-care, and renewal. Since the Sun governs energy, Sunday is ideal for reflecting on goals. Pursue activities that replenish you and set intentions for the week. Use this day to nurture your inner light and connect with your true self. As the Sun rises to illuminate the day, use this time to reignite your passion and vision for growth.

Moon ☽

The Moon is Earth's only natural light at night, and it changes phases as it orbits Earth. In astrology, the Moon represents our feelings, inner world, intuition, and the idea of a Mother or a maternal figure. While the Sun shows who we are on the outside, the Moon shines light on our emotional side, shaping how we care for others and find comfort. She helps us feel emotionally safe.

The Moon creates a calming connection in the night, offering light in the darkness and connecting the mystical with a comforting presence. She reflects our emotions and surfaces feelings that might otherwise remain hidden. Her presence guides us to seek meaning and comfort even in shadows, inviting deep self-exploration. Whether crescent or full, waning or waxing, the Moon observes like a wise mother, offering us understanding to those facing emotional trials and tribulations.

The Moon rules the sign Cancer, known for deep feelings, thoughtful nature, and close ties to home and to the past. If the Moon is strong in your chart, you might have a stronger intuition and an overwhelming need for emotional bonds. On the other hand, tough Moon aspects can mean more mood swings or trouble with handling your feelings. The main point is to recognize how you manage emotions, not whether you experience them.

The Sun stays in each sign for about a month, but the Moon changes its sign every two to three days and finishes all twelve signs in about 28 days. This quick movement reveals her ever-changing nature of emotions and her strong influence on our shifting feelings. If you feel your mood change with the Moon, these quick shifts may be why. I know a few people who are heavily affected emotionally when the moon is full. If you are one of those people, too, make sure to allow yourself time to let out a good cry and then maybe take a nice, relaxing bath. You deserve it!

In your birth chart, the Moon shows how you handle feelings, what makes you feel secure, how you care for others, and the relationship with your mother or mother figure. The sign and house reveal your emotional style and where you find fulfillment, helping you see where you shine emotionally.

If your Moon is in the 4th house, you emotionally process things in a Cancerian way, as someone deeply connected to their family and roots. You feel better at home, being all cozied up! You likely find comfort in nostalgic experiences that take you back and familiar surroundings where you can be yourself. You might prioritize your emotional security above other things. You could be someone very protective of your family.

Alternatively, if your Moon is in the 10th house, your feelings and work life are connected. You may find happiness in public praise or moving up in your career. Working hard and caring about your reputation can push you, but it can also bring stress and make you worry about your job.

To further illustrate the Moon's influence, she governs Monday, a day for reflection, sensitivity, and restoration. Because the Moon guides the subconscious mind, Mondays are ideal for planning, self-care, and processing emotions, not necessarily taking on new projects; it's more of a go with the flow energy. Knowing your Moon sign can guide you in discovering what brings you emotional fulfillment.

Mercury ☿

Your quick-witted, fast-talking friend Mercury is always ready to spill the latest tea. Not only can Mercury tell it like it is, but it can also pick up new languages and navigate social circles effortlessly. Mercury adapts easily and learns, almost as fast as they talk, which is almost instantly. Their energy is restless and chaotic; they often overthink and tend to blurt things out before filtering their thoughts. Mercury's playful vibe means they also get easily overwhelmed, and you might, too, depending on your own energy level.

In planetary terms, Mercury is the smallest of all the planets and the fastest, too. Mercury moves closest to the Sun and completes a full circle in only 88 Earth days' time. This makes total sense when you consider how Mercury can represent being quick, intelligent, technologically advanced, and fast traveling. When Mercury moves in, everything speeds up: your thoughts, conversations, travel plans, and when Mercury retrograde hits, a bit of chaos follows.

In astrology, Mercury rules how you think, speak, write, and make sense of the world around you. It's your inner voice and how you can understand experiences and process information. It's how you can share your thoughts with others. Mercury rules two of the zodiacal signs, Gemini and Virgo. This energy could manifest in various ways in your life, including curiosity, adaptability, and critical thinking. Depending on the sign, it can break down in different ways. For example, in Gemini, the vibe is more playful and outwardly expressive. In Virgo, that energy is more focused and analytical. You know how the Moon can show you how you feel, Mercury tells you how you can communicate and understand the feelings of others.

When Mercury is stationed directly, your thoughts will come naturally and flow easily. Your ideas will cling to you, and connections are made organically. Multitasking is second nature, and this makes it easy to get things done, just like Mercury loves. But when Mercury turns retrograde, everything tends to slow down drastically. Misunderstandings become the norm, technology doesn't work like it once did, making plans and then following through are difficult, and we often find ourselves revisiting a time where we felt uncomfortable before (for some, an unwanted ex may show up). This is just a lesson for you where Mercury is asking you to reflect on this moment, not do anything drastic, and realign your actions so you can learn from the past and hopefully, fingers crossed, not make the same mistakes again.

I've noticed that Mercury retrograde tends to hit those with strong Mercury placements the hardest, whether that's a Virgo Rising, Sun, or Moon, or a Gemini Rising, Sun, or Moon. While Mercury retrograde affects everyone in some way, if you have one of these placements, you might find that things just don't work as they usually do. It can feel like the world is off balance, and during this time, it can be frustrating, to say the least. Personally, I experience the most difficulties during this time, and I think it is because I have Virgo Rising. I'm curious whether others with similar placements experience it too.

The position of Mercury in your birth chart reveals how you think, converse with others, and how you process information. It will show your learning style, how you express yourself best, and the way your mind works. The zodiac sign Mercury falls under influences your communication style and whether you're sharp, detail-oriented, able to multitask, intuitive, or analytical. The house placement shows where this mental energy is focused and in what areas of life you like to share and gather knowledge. Together, the sign and house of Mercury add insight into how you connect with others and where your thoughts are most influenced.

If your Mercury is in the 2nd house, your thought processing and communication style are closely tied to your view of what security and material comfort mean to you. You might constantly think about your financial future, or you might enjoy discussing ways to increase your wealth, how you work, your possessions, or even investments that you have stock in. You probably process information in a practical and grounded way, since the second house is ruled by Taurus, which is ruled by Venus. You may find mental peace in securing your physical world, and you may feel a deep connection to the things you own, especially if they hold sentimental value or personal meaning.

If Mercury is in your 11th house, your thoughts are constantly in motion, often sparked by connections with others. You want to contribute to the greater good, and you process information best when you're networking, whether on social media, with friends, or in your community. You thrive in conversations when you are talking about your hopes and dreams, especially with like-minded people. Your communication often centers on out-of-the-box ideas and social causes. You may root for the underdog, seeing potential that others don't. Intellectual conversations inspire you; small talk seldom does.

Mercury is associated with Wednesday, the middle of the week, and a day that thrives on productivity, learning, and writing. This is the best time to have those important conversations you may have been holding off on or to learn something new that you have always felt curious about studying. Understanding where Mercury lives in your birth chart can offer insight into how you think, learn, speak, and connect with others, and how you can best channel your own voice.

Venus ♀

She is the epitome of love, joy, happiness, and a touch of luxury. Venus knows how to have a good time and keep things light. She likes to feel good, whether that's through delicious food, a fun concert, wearing a beautiful outfit, or being warm and snuggly in her California King-sized bed, with Egyptian cotton sheets and her silk pajamas on. She's soft, indulgent, and maybe just a little bit bougie (not on a budget). But it's not just about the material stuff with Venus, it's all about the experience. Is the vibe... vibing? She loves to feel either emotionally or physically. She wants that connection. She's the flirty gesture, the heartfelt love letter, the romantic playlist. And if she feels like she is not being appreciated? She'll find it elsewhere with someone who will.

In planetary terms, Venus moves leisurely, much slower compared to fast-action Mercury. She is not far from the Sun herself; in fact, she is the second planet to the Sun and is known for her incredible heat. Venus is often seen as the warm and loving planet. It makes perfect sense: Venus rules over what we cherish in life, how we show love to others (romantically or platonically), and how we attract people, places, or things. Obviously, she also influences what we consider beauty.

Venus is the planet of harmonious things, physical pleasure, romance, art, music, and money. Imagine this: an expensive dinner at a lavish restaurant, followed by a romantic serenade, then going home in a luxurious car to your mansion of a home, and then getting all comfortable in bed after a nice steaming hot shower with all the bells and whistles involved. Sounds nice, huh?

In astrology, Venus rules two zodiacal signs, Taurus and Libra. This fusion of signs gives her some reach. She behaves differently with each sign: with Taurus, she's more grounded, sensual, and loyal, desiring comfort, touch, and a slow-burning type of love. With Libra, she expresses herself through charm and aesthetics; Venus in Libra is like a gentle voice sharing poetry, creating an inviting and beautiful atmosphere. Wherever Venus appears in your chart, she teaches you what you love, how you love it, and how you want to be loved in return.

When Venus is directly aligned, the vibe is natural and flowing. You feel tapped into your magnetism with people and relationships. Opportunities come, joy surfaces, and peace is found. You can express your affection for others with ease. You might find joy in everything you do. However, when Venus turns retrograde, the energy shifts suddenly. Your love life can feel altered. Your acne can overpower your face. Music that once brought joy can start to irritate you, and that's just the beginning.

You might start rethinking what you really value in life (and who really values you). This is a time (like Mercury retrograde) to watch out for Exes and people you cut off way back when who are heading your way. Unresolved issues or wounds from the past can resurface quickly, leaving you to clean up emotional messes you thought were long gone. Your self-worth is being tested now. It's like your homegirl Venus is asking, "Are you being true to yourself about what brings you joy and happiness?"

Venus retrograde hits Libra or Taurus Risings, Suns, or Moons hard. You may notice extreme shifts in love, money, or your appearance. In your birth chart, Venus reveals your personal style, love language, money habits, and relationship needs. Her sign shapes whether you seek passion, stability, freedom, or emotional depth. The house shows where your love and worth express themselves.

For example, if Venus is in your 5th house, love feels like a movie or theatrical performance, and you are the star. You crave romance that's fun, bold, and maybe a little dramatic (much like Venus in Leo). You might be a big flirt, love to date, or enjoy creating art. You want to give and receive love warmly and charmingly. You may be the type to show off your partner to others and be very proud of them. You probably have a grandiose way of showing people in your one-on-one relationships how much they mean to you.

If Venus is in your 6th house, you often express love through acts of service. You might enjoy supporting others, making their lives easier, or simply being there consistently for your loved ones. Finding joy in daily routines can turn ordinary activities into meaningful connections, especially when shared with others. Tasks that others see as mundane can feel comforting or even pampering when done for someone you care about. This placement often aligns with Virgo Venus energy, love that's gentle, practical, and thoughtfully organized. It's not loud, but it's dependable, consistent, giving, and always present in daily life.

Venus rules Friday, the day of beauty, pleasure, and love. It's great for self-care or planning a date. Since it's payday for many, take a moment to check your bank balance with intention and gratitude. Venus isn't just a romantic; she makes life feel beautiful, enjoyable, fun, and worth living. She is that girl! Or guy! Either way, she is just happy to thrive!

Mars ♂

Mars is that friend who can't sit still. Always ready to go, basically anywhere, and is down for literally anything. Mars has no chill. Mars won't let you sit back and take your time; Mars wants to get things done. While this energy can be a bit exhausting, Mars is also quick to stand up for what matters most. Driven, bold, and sometimes hostile, this sign is never passive-aggressive or lazy.

Mars is that intense energy you feel when you're fired up. It could be anger, passion, lust, or even ambition, but whichever way it shows up for you, you feel it immensely. Mars gives off a lot of masculine energy. He isn't someone who comes into a room quietly; you can hear him coming from down the hall, charging into the room, and is ready to get shit done.

Mars is action first. He does not like to wait, and while that can be super motivating, it can also lead to impulsive decisions or burnout if not checked. Mars is a planet we all need. He is part of our inner warrior. He is the one who gives us courage and fuel when we don't feel so courageous and reminds us that sometimes, to get what we want, we must fight for it.

Mars, the red planet, is named after the Roman god of war. This connection fits, given Mars's fiery hue and ambiance. Mars symbolizes fighting, energy, and heat. He's the first planet beyond Earth not known for kindness. Mars's position in your chart shows where you're most reactive or assertive, and which life areas this energy affects. Mars is smaller than Earth, but I wouldn't underestimate it. (He does carry a bit of Napoleon syndrome.) He's quick, and his rotation spins with urgency.

In astrology, this planet connects to our internal drive, our sexuality, external and internal conflict, and how we pursue what we want in life without feeling held back. Mars rules Aries, the bold 'act now, think later' sign, and traditionally rules Scorpio, which adds intensity, control, and power. When Mars is activated in your chart, you might feel persistent, energized, or ready to fight for your desires, or just wanting to fight period, depending on the sign and reasoning. However, when Mars is uncontrollable and unmanageable, anger issues arise, passive-aggression stirs, or complete burnout can appear unexpectedly.

When Mars moves direct, motivation tends to flow. You may find it easier to assert yourself, pursue goals, or finally speak your mind. You might feel more confident in your body and more connected to your sexuality. Mars can energize you to act and overcome anything in your way.

The opposite happens when Mars retrogrades. It's like your inner battery struggles and dies. You are the cell phone with 1% battery life. Your energy might feel zapped, your rage may simmer below the surface, and everything you usually can push and power through suddenly feels like a struggle from hell. When Mars retrogrades, the universe is asking you to reevaluate how and when you use your energy. Mars retrograde affects Aries and Scorpio placements the most, sometimes making it feel as if their inner drive is diminished. During this phase, you might notice that your usual passion has cooled or that old disputes have resurfaced. This period is about reflection and tolerance; traits Mars doesn't naturally favor.

In your birth chart, Mars represents your assertive side, drive, approach to conflict, and sexual energy. It reveals what you pursue, desire, and how you respond to challenges. Some people enjoy a challenge; others do not. The zodiac sign Mars occupies colors how your motivation appears. Is it bold like Leo or Aries? Strategic like Capricorn or Virgo? Or quietly assertive and emotionally charged like Pisces?

The house Mars falls in will show where you naturally assert yourself and where your energy is most directed. To get a closer look, let's look at a couple of examples: If Mars is in your 10th house, your ambition and what drives you are naturally tied to your career and public life. You're probably someone who is driven by success, your achievements, and making your mark in this world. You will climb that business ladder and not look back. It's something you feel like you must do, and you probably don't mind a challenge, even if that means proving yourself to others. You work hard and are bold in professional settings, and your coworkers/employers know you as a competitive professional. In fact, you may even be the boss at your job.

If Mars is found in your 4th house, your home life may feel like a battlefield. Family dynamics could have been intense; you might have had some angry parental units in the home, or the dynamic could have just always been heated. It may have felt like home was a place of walking on eggshells because at any moment, everything might just blow up. This could show up in your adult life as a need to protect your home or assert yourself in your personal space. Sometimes, with this placement, domestic life isn't peaceful or quiet, but more tense and passionate. It's giving warrior energy when protecting loved ones or the home. You may have felt like you had to be the fighter in some sort of fashion; if it wasn't others fighting in front of you, they were fighting against you.

Mars is associated with Tuesday, which is a great day to get things done. Do you ever find yourself doing more on Tuesdays than you might have on Mondays? Well, if your answer is yes, there is some logic to this. Mondays really aren't the best day to get things done or start your week. Planning your week, yes, doing all the tasks? No. Tuesdays are ruled by motivation and movement. Tuesday is perfect for tackling something that's been waiting to be checked off your to-do list, hitting up that high-intensity class that you have thought about getting into, or immersing yourself in something physical. Clean the house, walk the dog, do some yoga, scream it out, get pissed off, listen to some angry music. Tuesday is built for that energy, and it can be beneficial if used that way.

Jupiter ♃

Now, it's time to talk about Jupiter. This is your free-spirited bestie who is eager to see the world and learn everything about it. Jupiter has bigger-than-life energy and is all about hyping you up. This planet is literally your biggest cheerleader. It's the friend who encourages you not only to dream big but to take action and make it happen. Jupiter is always looking for and reaching toward more. It can be in philosophy, religion, travel, or whatever they pursue to find true meaning in whatever "it" is.

Jupiter doesn't just walk into a room and sit; their presence fills up the space. This planet always looks on the bright side and can be optimistic to a fault. If they get knocked down, they get up and keep going. Jupiter is all about growth, intelligence, raw honesty, and a love of exploring both nearby and distant worlds. They're always ready to embark on a new adventure. Jupiter is your closest friend, life coach, and motivational speaker in one planet.

Jupiter is full of inspiring, seize-the-day energy that can motivate us all. Like anything, it can sometimes overextend itself, making promises it can't keep or jumping into decisions too quickly. Jupiter, with all its might, has its limits and can sometimes be overly positive. But that's what makes the universe so fascinating! Moderation and small doses aren't its style. Jupiter thrives on more in all it does and encourages growth wherever it appears in your chart.

In planetary terms, Jupiter is the largest planet in our solar system, and in astrology, its energy is just as powerful. Jupiter doesn't aim for small; if it did, it would just go home, which it refuses to do. It wants to explore, expand, and enlighten those around it, as well as to be enlightened itself. That's why it's the planet of higher learning, long-distance travel, philosophy, abundance, luck, wishes, and spiritual beliefs. Jupiter can be the traveler, the teacher, the preacher, or the monk, and the lucky charm we all need rolled into one.

For Jupiter, it's about belief systems, whether religious or personal, and how they shape the way you live. Jupiter brings blessings, though in the form of money, good grades, longevity, wisdom, or travel. Sometimes, your most significant growth comes from simple experiences, whether they seem good or bad to you, that guide your spirit to move forward.

Jupiter rules Sagittarius and co-rules Pisces, tying it closely to spirituality and wisdom. Strong Jupiter placements make you curious and open-minded, encouraging you to explore life's biggest mysteries. Yet, when Jupiter's energy is overdone, it can lead to overindulgence, impulsiveness, bluntness, and utter arrogance. Ultimately, Jupiter acts as your inner wise guy, urging you to take risks and trust your path.

When Jupiter is going direct, it feels like everything in life is falling into place. The universe itself whispers to you "yes" more often than "no." Opportunities flow freely, your mindset feels expansive and optimistic, and life seems to open doors for you. Dreams appear to be coming true, but when Jupiter goes retrograde, it's time to slow down. This is when things start to shift, and you'll notice that you are being prompted to reflect on what your beliefs truly are. What are you genuinely grateful for? During this retrograde, Jupiter encourages you to look inward and consider whether you are aligning with your dreams and making the most of life. Jupiter retrograde isn't always very dramatic; as it might sound, it is more about deep philosophical reflection, prompting you to think from within.

If you are fortunate enough to have Jupiter in your 8th house, your gifts often come through life's layers of change. Blessings are found here through intimacy. You can grow spiritually and emotionally by engaging in shadow work, therapy, or by confronting emotional truths directly. You handle loss differently from others; you may experience it more frequently, which might spark your interest in related topics. You're naturally attracted to life's mysteries: the occult, psychology, or metaphysics. You might believe in rebirth after loss and in the idea that we have all been part of each other's lives before, interwoven. There's also a fortunate aspect to how you manage other people's finances. With Jupiter in the 8th, you could receive abundant financial support through joint partnerships or inheritances. Jupiter here bestows upon you depth, helping you trust your intuition, which guides you to breakthroughs throughout your life. You're the type to uncover hidden wisdom when experiencing a crisis; more than likely, that is how this will activate for you.

Having Jupiter in the 11th house truly puts you in a special place because you're both a dreamer and a doer! You're the one who brings ideas to life, especially when it comes to your future goals and the wonderful people you connect with. This placement makes you a natural visionary, always thinking ten steps ahead and feeling energized when working in groups, participating in online communities, or supporting causes you believe in. You're often surrounded by friends, allies, mentors, and collaborators who help open doors to exciting new opportunities. You likely have a genuine faith in humanity and plenty of big ideas for making the world better for everyone. Sometimes, your optimistic outlook can even be a touch idealistic. But when you're with the right people, that's when you really thrive. Whether it's starting a movement you believe in, building a sustainable brand, or working with your close friends, you're shaping a brighter future through making meaningful connections.

Jupiter is linked to Thursday, the day dedicated to learning and inspiration. Thursdays are the perfect time to take a class you've always considered trying. It's also a good moment to share your truth with others, whether that's with your partner, family, best friend, your dog, or on social media; luck is in your favor. Sometimes, it might be something simple like expressing gratitude for what you're thankful for: your house, job, car, children, or whatever you are happy to have. Random Thought: Since Thursday is the day we talk about our blessings, it makes sense that Thanksgiving occurs on a Thursday, too.

Saturn ♄

He remains calm and collected, gently guiding us through challenging lessons. Saturn symbolizes discipline in the zodiac, presenting us with challenges that foster our growth into our true selves. A wise man whose advice might not be appreciated at first but eventually becomes valued. He offers guidance in a soft, almost whispering manner. His approach is strong yet gentle, earning respect through quiet confidence rather than loud commands.

He can be a bit harsh, insisting that you complete your daily chores or tasks before you're allowed to go outside and enjoy your life, or he can act like a strict Ms. Trenchible, making life feel rigid, suffocating, and not fun at all. However, through his presence, Saturn encourages you to be reliable and committed to earning the things you want in life. He does this by influencing your life through karma and discipline, and by dedicating yourself to something over a long period of time rather than being flighty and quick.

Saturn, in our solar system, is the sixth planet from the Sun and is most famous for the stunning rings that truly make it stand out in the sky. It spins quickly on its axis, yet it takes an amazing 29.5 years for Saturn to orbit the Sun. With over 140 moons, it's also less dense than water, which I find really fascinating. Despite its massive size and commanding presence, Saturn is light enough to float. It's a beautiful reminder that, even when something seems heavy and serious, there's often an element of mystery and wonder. To me, that's just poetic.

In astrology, Saturn appears as the wise, authoritative figure, full of responsibility, structure, and boundaries. He doesn't rush; in fact, he takes his sweet, sweet time when it comes to letting you enjoy the rewards of your hard work. Saturn rules your career, long-term goals, and the legacy you're building. He reveals upcoming challenges, not to discourage you, but to make you stronger. Often feared for his tough love, Saturn is here to help you create something lasting and something more substantial than a passing idea, a temporary relationship, or a fleeting dream. He wants you to be grounded, self-reliant, and prepared. Yes, he causes delays and holds you to higher standards than other planets, but only so you can become clear about what you truly want and what's truly worth it.

When he returns to his original position in your birth chart, it's called your Saturn Return, and it signals a major coming-of-age period, usually around your 29th or 30th birthday. That's why many people change careers, end relationships, move across the country, start or finish college, or completely reevaluate their purpose during this time. It's Saturn's way of asking, "Is this the life I really want?"

If the answer is no, he'll guide you gently or more firmly toward a path that feels right for you. His energy might feel heavy or chaotic at times, depending on what needs to change, but everything is aimed at achieving harmony. Although society often marks adulthood at 18, Saturn reminds us that true maturity usually comes closer to 30. This phase calls for maturity, strength, and responsibility. By embracing your lessons and facing challenges head-on, you'll gain wisdom and stability, building a solid foundation for your future.

Saturn governs the sign of Capricorn, and traditionally also rules Aquarius. In Capricorn, Saturn is like a tough boss climbing the ladder, emphasizing discipline and leaving a strong legacy. In Aquarius, he adopts a more intellectual and societal role, focusing on innovation within structure and on responsibility toward the collective.

If you have strong Saturn placements in your chart, you might be someone with an old soul, carrying yourself with quiet determination and resilience. You could be very goal-oriented, but also gentle with yourself if things don't go as planned. When Saturn's aspects are challenging in your chart, it's common to feel like you're battling feelings of inadequacy, a fear of failure, or an overwhelming pressure to be perfect. Remember, growth happens when you realize that Saturn isn't here to punish you; instead, it's here to help shape you into the wonderful person you're meant to become.

If your Saturn is in the 6th house, work is serious business for you. You don't go to work to play; you go to achieve. You feel the weight of responsibility in your daily routines, your health, and how you can serve others. You probably take on more than you can handle and constantly feel the pressure. You feel like you have something to prove in the workplace or through your productivity, but as you get older, this role increasingly becomes a gift. It teaches you that endurance, precision, and the quiet mastery gained from showing up day after day are worth it. You have the potential to become a true expert or even a legend in your field, not because it's easy, but because you never give up.

If Saturn is in your 7th house, your relationships carry karmic significance. Your partnerships won't be simple or casual. Earlier in your life, relationships might have seemed to you like rejection, loneliness, or even the fear of falling in love or committing. As you mature, Saturn in the 7th house teaches you how to develop meaningful relationships. These are relationships based on mutual respect, demonstrate maturity, and have the potential to be long-term. If you have this placement, you're learning how to build lasting love.

Saturn is linked to Saturday, a day that's all about structure, realignment, and practical action. It's a time when many of us happily catch up on chores we've been putting off, organize our homes to create calmer, more peaceful spaces, and tend to responsibilities that slipped through during the busy week. But once the to-do list is checked off, Saturday provides a wonderful opportunity for well-deserved fun and relaxation. This sweet balance is the soul of what Saturn teaches us: work hard first, and the rewards will come.

This makes me smile a little inside because it reflects on how I was raised. Literally every Saturday morning, my mom and I would clean our house, and then we were free to go out and have fun. It was how she was brought up, too. When I learned that Saturn was linked to Saturday and understood what it all really meant, it all clicked for me. Knowing where Saturn is in your birth chart can show where your soul is meant to grow.

It might be where you feel most stuck at first, but it's also where you can become the strongest.

Don't worry about Saturn; there's no need to be afraid of it. It doesn't imply that everything will be tough in the house it occupies. Instead, think of this planet as a helpful guide that balances out what is truly meant for you and supports your long-term growth in that area. It's not your enemy at all, but rather a part of your journey to stability.

Uranus ♅

Uranus is like that unpredictable friend who's not just a genius but also surprises you with wild ideas during brunch. Sometimes, they might vanish for six months and then suddenly pop back up with a half-shaved head, new tattoos, and surprise... a Nobel Prize in something totally unexpected and offbeat! This friend is wonderfully eccentric and rebellious, caring little about rules or fitting in. They're not here to follow anyone's game; they'll do their own thing, and if someone tries to stand in their way, they'll find a way to move forward. They're not into conforming. Tell them they can't do something, and they'll only want it more. Unlike other planets, Uranus isn't into tradition unless it's about shaking things up. That's really the spirit of Uranus.

In planetary terms, Uranus is an outer planet, which means it moves very slowly. It is far from the sun and takes about 84 years to complete one orbit. Uranus spends roughly 7 years in each zodiac sign. Because of this, it is considered a generational planet. So, if you and someone else were born in the same year, there's a high chance you have Uranus in the same sign; the only difference is their rising sign, which would cause this planet to appear in a different house on their chart. I'll go into that more later when we discuss houses and explore examples.

In astrology, Uranus is the inventor and the rebel; whether it has a cause, Uranus is the one who shakes things up a bit. Uranus is in it for the long haul because wherever it is, it tends to stay there for quite a while. Uranus thinks outside the box and with precision. He isn't about rushing to get things done quickly like Mercury; instead, he asks, "What will shock them the most?" He aims to push you toward freedom and break any cycles you're stuck in. He encourages you to root for the underdog and develop your own unique ideas. This planet is all about evolution and doing whatever it takes to achieve it.

Uranus rules the sign of Aquarius, which makes perfect sense when you think about it, because Aquarius is the sign that thinks ten to twenty years ahead. It seeks independence, growth, and a connection with the collective and groups, including friends, but on its own unpredictable terms. It likes to do things its own way. Don't expect it to follow rules or directions; those are the first things it ignores. It prefers to start from scratch and create something entirely on its own, finding new ways to make it work faster, easier, and more efficiently. This planet governs individualism, the world of technology, and major breakthroughs, so when it moves through different houses (or depending on where it is naturally in yours), it can make you go, "WTH just happened?" It's all part of its master plan to help us evolve and become more than we currently are.

When Uranus is moving directly, it's like a sudden awakening of clarity here to shake you out of your routine. Suddenly, you might feel like quitting your job, moving somewhere random, and on a whim, just starting over in a new chapter of your life. It's okay that everything flipped upside down. That's Uranus's probing mind saying to itself, "Let's see what this button does and that button…oh, and this one." Suddenly, you feel pulled to break free of societal norms and are excited to stand up for something new and cause-worthy. But when Uranus goes retrograde, that energy that makes you feel rebellious goes inside. You could begin to question the things you are so determined to break free from. When this planet goes retrograde, you might wonder if these changes you are making are for the right reasons and whether this will be beneficial for the collective as a whole.

People with a strong Uranian energy in their charts often see themselves as the unique "black sheep" of their families or as the inventive visionaries among their friends. They tend to be ahead of their time, cherishing independence and original thinking, and they don't like feeling confined or limited. If Uranus is conjunct your Sun, Moon, or Ascendant, you probably resist being told what to do and value your rebellious spirit. You naturally seek freedom and can get restless when things become too predictable and mundane. Your life might be full of sudden, unexpected moments that can be both exciting and a bit chaotic, but each one offers a chance to learn more about who you truly are.

The house where Uranus appears is where you might experience a desire to break free or start a revolution. If Uranus is in the 4th house, your home life and family may not follow traditional paths. You could have had an unconventional upbringing, felt the urge to move frequently, maybe you even created your own unique version of what family is, or chose to live completely off-grid. Deep down, there's a strong need for freedom at your core, often rooted in your family experiences. You might even be the one to break the cycle in your family line, whether that involves overcoming generational curses or making a clean break from repeating patterns.

If Uranus is in your 7th house, your relationships won't follow the usual pattern. You might attract unique or freedom-loving partners or experience sudden breakups or makeups. Your love life will be quite fascinating, to say the least. You might think outside the box with your partnerships and relationships, well beyond what social norms expect. You're learning how to be in an alliance without losing your sense of self. Polygamy? Age-gap relationships? Long-distance soulmates? Uranus doesn't care how strange it seems to others, as long as it's genuine and aligns with your beliefs.

Neptune ♆

Neptune is your spiritual friend who reminds you of a creative psychic hippie, one who is totally in touch with their emotions, loves to daydream, and vanishes into thin air after saying something poetic and soul-stirring. This is the friend who then reappears several months later, having joined a spiritual retreat in Bali and now claiming to be clairvoyant, along with a starving artist. This friend speaks in metaphors and has the eyes of someone who's seen other dimensions. They are deep. They're mysterious, dreamy, and completely uninterested in anything mundane. They don't like to be rushed and find being alone appealing. Neptune doesn't live in the "real world." He's just visiting here.

Neptune is an outer planet that moves slowly but has a reflective influence. It takes 165 years to orbit the zodiac, spending about 14 years in each sign. Along with Uranus, Neptune is called a generation planet, meaning people born around the same time (or within roughly 14 years) share the same Neptune sign. Still, its impact varies depending on the individual chart and the rising signs. This sign plays a role in shaping how we, as a collective, approach spirituality.

Neptune reveals itself in a mysterious way. This planet symbolizes the mystic, the dreamer, the illusionist, and the artist. Neptune brings a renewed energy, pulling you into visions filled with symbols and emotions that are hard to put into words. It encourages belief in dreams and deeper connections to the world beyond what most see. Governing spirituality, dreams, fantasies, art, music, and mysticism, Neptune can also lead to delusion and illusion. Escapism often emerges during spiritual awakenings or simply as a common theme here. Neptune urges you to see beyond the obvious, but be careful not to lose yourself while seeking your true self.

Neptune governs Pisces, who are known for their intuition, empathy, and the tendency to blur boundaries. It weaves together stories of confusion, the mysterious underworld, fairy tales, deception, hidden things, and addictions. This planet reminds us that it's easy to view life through rose-colored glasses. Ultimately, it's our own responsibility to distinguish what is real from what is not. When Neptune is prominent in our charts, these boundaries can become a bit blurry.

When Neptune moves directly, it encourages our creativity, sparks our imagination, and deepens our exploration of spirituality. You might find yourself feeling more connected to your dreams or more open to empathy and creative ideas. But when Neptune goes retrograde, our inspirations, feelings, and creativity temporarily turn inward. We might realize that what we once believed to be true is actually an illusion, and then we start to fall apart. This can lead you to question your beliefs and see things in a new light.

People with strong Neptune placements, like Neptune conjunct the Sun, Moon, or Ascendant, often feel like they come from another world because they sense they're different from others. They might notice that they're very artistic, highly sensitive, or naturally talented psychics. These qualities feel very real to them. They can easily pick up on the emotions in a room. Sometimes, they find it hard to set boundaries or distinguish between reality and fantasy. Spending time alone helps them recharge mentally and energetically. They believe in finding peace within their spirituality or religious beliefs. They need a way to express their imagination and creativity. Without this outlet, they might keep everything inside, struggle with addiction, get involved in toxic relationships, or feel constantly uncomfortable and overwhelmed, wanting to escape from the suffocation of anything that feels too confining or structured.

If Neptune is in your 2nd house, you might find your feelings about money and values are a bit fuzzy or idealized. Your income could go up and down, and you could be very generous or drawn to making money through art or healing. You need to explore what actual value really means, including your own worth, and to stay grounded without being misled by dreams of success.

Having Neptune in your 11th house can add a gentle touch of mystery to your friendships and community. You might find yourself drawn to spiritual or artistic friends, and it can be a delightful challenge to see what really resonates with your true self. Sometimes, your hopeful ideas about what the world needs can lead to disappointment when things don't turn out as you'd hoped. During these moments, you might also encounter friends who aren't quite who you thought they might be, aren't fully honest, or your community might feel different than what you expected it would.

Pluto ♀ or ♇

The last planet we consider in astrology is Pluto. Pluto is the planetary friend who says, "Let's talk about dying," in a coffee shop on a random Wednesday morning, as if it's no big deal or anything. Then, without hesitation, it dives into topics like trauma dumping, life after death (like Neptune, but darker), and it adds a touch of rising-from-the-ashes energy. Speaking of Wednesday, this planet gives off some major Wednesday Adam vibes. They see through everyone's BS and aren't interested in small talk. They want to go deep and stay intrigued. If they sense anything trivial or shallow, they are turned off and won't believe you (or want to talk to you) again. Having faced the dark side of life multiple times, they really don't care if you don't like them.

Pluto is the farthest of the traditional planets we've talked about before. It moves quite slowly, taking about 248 years to go around the Sun. It spends between 15 and 26 years in each zodiac sign, so it really represents a generational planet. Because of this, your Pluto sign can reveal the hidden aspects of yourself that you're here to change into something new and better. Meanwhile, Pluto's placement in your chart highlights the areas where this deep work is taking place. Pretty fascinating.

Pluto symbolizes death, rebirth, dominance, control, trauma, and renovation. It's a mysterious and powerful force that encourages us to let go of falsehoods, clearing away what no longer serves us, and find new beginnings. While Pluto's energy can be intense and challenging at times, it's ultimately life-changing. It governs what we tend to hide or suppress, bringing those feelings and things into the light for healing and growth.

Pluto rules over Scorpio, and like that zodiac sign, he is eager to uncover the truth, no matter how cold or uncomfortable it might be. Pluto shows us that true power isn't about control; it's about submission, facing our own darkness, and reclaiming our inner strength. People strongly influenced by Pluto often go through intense life experiences and karmic relationships, and may witness significant endings or challenges, revealing emotional depths that most people can't even fathom. But they also possess the incredible ability to heal and empower others by first healing themselves. Doing shadow work is a natural expression of Pluto or Scorpio energy. It involves exploring the darkest, saddest, or most hidden parts of ourselves and addressing issues at their root to heal and move on.

When Pluto is direct, its energy feels outward and energizing. This might make you feel more ready to take control of your destiny or face challenges more directly. When Pluto is in retrograde, the focus turns inward, and you might find yourself confronting your own fears. It's a powerful period of inner reflection and doing some shadow work, where you dig deep and reclaim what's been inside.

Suppose Pluto is strongly positioned in your chart, like conjunct your Sun, Moon, or Ascendant, you might come across as intense, attractive, intimidating, or even a little scary. You don't try to be, it just naturally shows. People can sense that you're honest and not easily manipulated, which might make them admire you or, at times, even fear you. Some might test your boundaries, but since you're influenced by water, you tend to let them learn their lessons the hard way by stepping back. You only forgive if it's truly needed, and often, that doesn't happen. Those with Pluto prominent in their chart walk through fire and renovate, constantly evolving and growing.

Your Pluto sign reveals your generation's key mission in life, highlighting themes of authority and revolution. The house where Pluto resides indicates the areas where you'll go through your most profound personal transformations. For instance, if Pluto is in your 3rd house, your words and thoughts carry significant weight, possibly even some psychic influence. You might have grown up in a challenging or secretive environment where open and honest communication was scarce. As you mature, you could become someone who speaks up about power, uncovers secrets, or writes down words that inspire and change others' lives. You may also have experienced healing from issues like gaslighting, gossip, jealousy, or verbal outbursts.

If Pluto is in your 10th house, your career journey promises to be unique and full of growth. You might find that your goals shift significantly over time, and your public image or even your relationship with authority could change. It's common to feel uncomfortable when others tell you what to do, but remember, your path may include rising to power or experiencing setbacks more than once. Embrace your mission and let go of the need to control how others perceive you, so your authentic self can shine brightly.

The Houses

Here is the part of astrology that pertains to "where" things are happening in your life. Houses are fascinating because they pull everything together. They tell us which sign is in each house and whether any planets are there, though not every house has a planet. That's perfectly okay! It doesn't mean you lack a certain house because you actually have all 12 houses that make up your unique birth chart. Astrology is full of layers, and this is just one more exciting piece to explore.

That's where the concept of quadrants really comes to life. Your birth chart is beautifully divided into four sections, each holding three houses. Think of each quadrant as representing a different meaningful area of your life.

The first quadrant (Houses 1–3) focuses on your personal identity and early experiences. The second (Houses 4–6) touches on your private life, daily routines, and acts of service. The third (Houses 7–9) connects you with others through relationships, beliefs, and adventures. The fourth quadrant (Houses 10–12) relates to your public life, your legacy, and your spiritual journey.

How do you know which sign rules each house? That depends on your birth time. Your birth time determines your rising sign, also called your Ascendant. This marks the start of your 1st house. Your rising sign is where your chart begins and influences the signs that rule each following house.

Starting from there, you'll notice the signs flow around the chart, moving counterclockwise. A specific sign guides each house, and even if some houses don't hold planets, they're still influenced by their ruling signs. This influence adds a special flavor and a touch of wabi-sabi to how the themes of each house appear in your life. While not every house might feel prominent right away, don't worry, each one has its own significance.

Let's get started at the beginning: The First House. Your entrance into the world, if you will.

1ˢᵗ House: The House of Self

Ruler: Aries

First Quadrant (Houses 1-3) Personal Development

The First House is ruled by Aries and governed by the fiery red planet Mars. This house marks the beginning of your entire birth chart. Located in the First Quadrant, it focuses on your personal growth and the core of your own unique identity. The First House starts with your Rising Sign, the zodiac sign that was appearing on the eastern horizon at the exact moment you were born. That's why your birth time is so important. Your Rising Sign sets the tone for your entire chart and acts as a lens through which you view the world. Think of it not as a mask, as some might say, but as your natural physical approach and how you present yourself in the world. It's often your first impression of your energy and vibe that other people see before they really get to know the real you. This house also represents early life on your personal wheel, where you begin to learn exactly who you are.

The First House is often called the House of Self because it shares the story of who you are. It reflects your identity, physical presence, character traits, instincts, and your first approach to life. This is how you naturally act, express yourself, and present yourself, whether through your clothing or how you carry yourself. It gives insight into how you start new things, such as projects, conversations, relationships, and travels. Focused entirely on you, this house is devoted completely to you. Every other house highlights a different area in your life; this is the start.

Planets in your First House really catch people's attention and highlight your personality and presence. Even if there aren't any planets here, your Rising Sign and other aspects to the Ascendant show how you see the world and how others perceive you.

Let's take a closer look at **Aries Rising**. If you have Aries rising in your chart, it means Mars is your ruling planet. Your second house is Taurus, and your third house is Gemini, with the rest following in that pattern. We're using the Whole Sign House System (we'll talk about Placidus later). As an Aries Rising, others see you as energetic, brave, and always ready to take action. You prefer to jump right into new experiences rather than wait around for permission. Your spirited energy is fast, straightforward, and sometimes a bit impatient, but that's just part of what makes you so charismatic.

You might have a naturally strong or athletic build, often giving off a lively vibe even if you're not into formal workouts. Your face could convey intensity or determination, with sharp eyes, a defined jawline, or striking features. Walking with a purpose, your movements are quick and confident. You might prefer wearing red tones, sporty styles, or simple outfits that let you move freely. Sometimes, people might find you a bit intimidating at first, not because you mean to be, but because of your self-assured presence. With Mars as your chart ruler, your drive and ambition truly shape who you are. The house and sign of Mars show where your energy is directed, how you approach conflicts, and what truly motivates you.

If Virgo is your rising sign from birth, Mercury rules your chart. Your second house is in Libra, and your third in Scorpio, following the Whole Sign system. As a **Virgo Rising**, you're often seen as thoughtful, perceptive, and detail-minded. There's a gentle, quiet confidence about you. You're not flashy, but you're sharp, quick-witted, and insightful. You come across as grounded, intelligent, and a bit reserved at first, until you open up. I get librarian and teacher vibes from Virgo risings.

You often find yourself scanning your surroundings and noticing the small details others might miss, which probably comes from a sense of alertness or readiness to act. You might have a neat and tidy look, even when you're dressed casually; your style feels both intentional and effortless. It's common to have slender, refined features or a petite, delicate frame. Many Virgo Risings prefer earth tones or a minimalist fashion sense. Your gaze is often sharp and analytical. Your movements tend to be precise and deliberate, and sometimes you're quick and energized by nervousness. Since Mercury rules your chart, your mind really shapes who you are. The placement of Mercury in your chart shows how you communicate, gather information, and how your thoughts influence your personality and decisions.

Let's explore **Scorpio Rising**! If you happen to have Scorpio as your rising sign, your chart is guided by Mars (the classic ruler) and Pluto (the modern ruler). Your second house touches Sagittarius, your third is in

Capricorn, and the journey continues. Scorpio Risings are often intense, mysterious, and incredibly magnetic. You might not say much at first, but people definitely sense your powerful presence. You tend to keep things private, sometimes become a bit defensive, and hold a firm stance, even when chaos is swirling beneath the surface. After social outings, you might find yourself needing some quiet time to recharge and process everything, which is completely natural.

There's a natural aura of strength and resilience about you that radiates. You might have captivating features, like soulful, ocean-blue eyes that seem to look right into others' hearts. Your facial expressions are often strong and distinctive, with a gentle hint of seriousness or depth. You might enjoy wearing dark or bold, edgy styles that perfectly match your unique personality. Your calm yet confident presence naturally draws respect and admiration. Your movements tend to be controlled and purposeful, reflecting a cautious trust in others. With Mars and Pluto influencing your chart, themes of transformation, intensity, and personal power are central to your life journey. Where these planets are positioned in your chart reveals what inspires you, how you embrace change, and where you find opportunities for deep growth or face challenges.

If you're a **Leo Rising**, the Sun rules your chart, giving you a natural glow that draws people in. Your second house is in Virgo, your third in Libra, and so on, creating a unique astrological map just for you, even if you're not trying to be the center of attention; you are. There's a genuine warmth and charm in you that makes others feel at ease. You carry yourself with a sense of purpose, as if you have important things to share or accomplish. Leadership and creative expression are incredible strengths that resonate with your lively spirit.

You might glow with a radiant or golden hue, or your skin or hair might have a sunny, cheerful quality. Think big hair, bold fashion choices, or a style that truly grabs attention. Whether you have curly, vibrant, or uniquely eccentric hair that makes a loud statement, you radiate confidence and stand tall. Your facial features brighten when you smile, your eyes are full of expression, and your wide grin lights up the room. There's often a touch of drama or flair in how you speak, walk, or dress, which adds to your magnetic personality. Since the Sun is your chart ruler, your sense of self is deeply connected to your purpose and natural creativity. The position of your Sun reveals what excites you, what your soul is longing for, and how you can step into your personal power and be recognized for who you truly are. This also emphasizes on how wonderfully you shine in your own unique way.

If you are a **Libra Rising** at your birth, Venus governs your chart, giving your second house in Scorpio and your third in Sagittarius. People with Libra Rising often come across as charming, graceful, and approachable. This likely gives off a pleasant, warm aura that makes others feel at ease around you. You probably have a keen artistic sense and value harmony in both your environment and your relationships. While you're naturally diplomatic, it doesn't mean you're a pushover; instead, you prefer balance over chaos, but you won't let others walk all over you.

When it comes to your appearance, you might have well-balanced or attractive facial features, perhaps with charming dimples or a warm, inviting smile. You could also have a passion for fashion or beauty that makes you look effortlessly stylish. Other lovely traits might include a gentle, soft voice or graceful body language, along with romantic or elegant touches to your wardrobe, such as floral patterns, silk fabrics, pinks, or pastel shades. All these details come together to create a vibe of someone who is naturally aware and well-mannered. With Venus as your chart ruler, your sense of self is beautifully connected to love, beauty, and connection. The placement of Venus in your chart reveals what draws you in, how you attract others, and how you bring harmony into your life.

When the **Sun** graces your **First House**, your personality truly shines with warmth and clarity. You'll notice that you radiate confidence and vitality, which often makes others see you as someone who is sure of themselves and comfortable in taking up space. There's a lovely sense of self-identity here, as you probably know who you are, or at least carry yourself as if you do. This placement naturally lends itself to leadership roles, especially since the Sun in the first house, ruled by Aries, highlights those qualities.

People may be drawn to your warmth, magnetism, and engaging presence. The only thing to watch out for? Sometimes you might be a bit self-focused, especially when you feel unnoticed. But overall, this placement really lights up your chart, bringing visibility to your personal journey and life energy.

In astrology, the Sun also symbolizes the father or a father figure, and having it in the first house suggests that this relationship often plays a vital role in shaping your confidence and identity, or how you present yourself to the world. It can be very empowering and inspiring, though challenges might sometimes lead to power struggles or ego conflicts. Many individuals with this placement exhibit noticeable physical and personality traits that reflect their father's influence. He might have been a bit temperamental, into physical training or some physical-related field, possibly a leader or in management.

With the **Moon** in your **First House**, your emotional inner world is closely connected to how you present yourself to others. You're sensitive, intuitive, and people often notice your mood before you even speak, just as you can sense theirs. You might come across as nurturing or emotionally available, someone who feels easy to open up to. Because the Moon's changing nature shifts your view of yourself and your presentation, this can be reflected in your appearance, emotions, and reactions to your environment. Likely, you radiate a gentle, approachable energy that others feel effortlessly.

Be mindful of how the moon's cycles influence you; the Moon can impact your energy, emotional processing, and intuition. Full moons, in particular, might strongly affect you, so make sure to stay grounded and carve out some personal time during those periods. In astrology, the Moon symbolizes the mother or maternal figure. Having it in the first house suggests you may have absorbed your mother's moods or felt her emotional presence deeply, almost as if her feelings became your own.

Sometimes, this points to a mother who was deeply caring and protective. At times, she may have been unpredictable, sensitive, or emotionally demanding, often teaching you early on to tune into others and read a room instinctively. Your bond with her might have been both comforting and overwhelming. As you grow older, learning to distinguish your own emotional patterns from those inherited from her becomes an integral part of your healing. This placement grants strong emotional intelligence and empathy; you naturally understand people's hearts. However, it also requires caring for yourself with the same compassion you give to others.

When **Mercury** lands in your **First House**, it really highlights how much your mind plays a role in shaping who you are. Your thoughts, words, curiosity, and mental processes all shine through your personality. Others often see you as lively, quick-witted, and intellectually alert, someone whose ideas and voice naturally stand out. You might have an expressive face and lively gestures that let people catch a glimpse of your thoughts or feelings even before you say a word.

This placement gives you a youthful, curious, and quick-thinking energy; you're always observing, analyzing, and making sense of the world around you. Since Mercury governs communication, sharing your thoughts and expressing yourself are key parts of your relationships. You're likely great at storytelling, teaching, writing, or public speaking, anything that lets you share your ideas. Often, conversations shape how you see yourself and your connections.

When you're passionate, you might talk for hours, inspiring and captivating others. On the flip side, if Mercury feels tense in your chart, you might overthink or hesitate before acting. Your mental energy can significantly influence your physical energy, too. When your mind is active, your body is too. You might find yourself restless, always pacing or fidgeting. It's also possible that from a young age, you were encouraged to ask questions or share your thoughts, which can be a delightful part of who you are.

When **Venus** is in the **First House**, you effortlessly come across as authentically attractive, no matter what traditional beauty standards might say. People are naturally drawn to your magnetic presence. You don't need to try hard or chase after attention; if it feels forced or unnatural, it's okay to pause. Authenticity should feel effortless. When you walk into a room, you're noticed, and your style often reflects your love for beauty.

Your energy tends to be soft, flirty, or simply pleasing, making others see you as lovely or captivating, even when you're just being yourself. This placement makes it easy for others to be drawn in by your charm, opening doors for you and creating personal connections. You're proud of what you love and tend to wear your heart on your sleeve, which only adds to your sincere allure. At times, though, you might become very aware of how others perceive you and feel pressure to look or act a certain way to maintain that sense of appeal.

Because Venus governs relationships and self-worth, this placement can sometimes lead you to seek validation through approval or affection.

You naturally want to be liked and can go out of your way to avoid conflict. Over time, you learn that your real power lies in being at peace with yourself, not in being perfect for others. There's also a strong creative streak here; you may express love through art, music, or simply by making your surroundings beautiful. Your presence tends to calm tension, and your warmth makes people feel seen and appreciated.

In childhood, you may have learned that being kind, cooperative, or pleasant helped you receive love, shaping how you approach connection now. As you grow, Venus here enables you to discover that your true beauty comes from self-acceptance and the love you radiate naturally.

When **Mars** is in the **First House**, you come across as strong-willed and confident. People see you as someone who knows what they want and isn't afraid to pursue it, which intensifies your presence. You move through life with an eagerness to embrace challenges at any moment. Your assertiveness and occasional impatience reflect an inner drive to get things done without waiting for permission or for others.

You tend to be straightforward and honest, preferring to face issues head-on and get everything out in the open. Sometimes, your strength might seem intimidating, but it's also what makes you so magnetic. You carry yourself with a sense of purpose, and others can sense that fierce determination even before you speak. You flourish when you have something to dedicate your energy to, whether it's work, fitness, or personal goals. You might have a natural love for movement or physical activity, as your energy often builds up in your body.

If not channeled constructively, that same fire can lead to restlessness or irritability. You may notice your temper flares quickly but also fades just as fast. Learning to direct your passion in healthy ways can help you avoid impulsive reactions or burnout. Sometimes, you might be passive-aggressive if you feel blocked or unheard, but when you learn to assert yourself calmly and clearly, your confidence becomes one of your strongest qualities.

This placement often points to a childhood where independence or self-assertion was emphasized early on; maybe you learned that standing up for yourself was necessary or that you had to fight to be heard. Over time, Mars here helps to shape that fired-up spirit into healthy self-leadership instead of defensiveness. People often perceive you as brave and unafraid of confrontation, even if you don't always feel that way inside.

When **Jupiter** is in your **First House**, it reflects a delightfully multifaceted personality. You might come across as charming, or even a bit exotic, drawing people in with your outgoing, approachable nature. You're wonderfully independent, filled with optimism, kindness, and a zest for life. It's no wonder you're considered a magnet for luck and often seem to have an insightful wisdom of various things.

This placement can give you fuller features or, in some cases, make you appear smaller; either way, the effects are pretty noticeable. Others likely see you as someone with fascinating stories, valuable lessons, or insights to share. Your personality is often vibrant, with a love for exploration, philosophy, different cultures, and continuous learning. Your personality is usually linked to your beliefs and your drive to pursue big dreams.

You may seem lucky, but it's because of your positive mindset and genuine curiosity. Your presence has a way of lifting those around you, as you naturally inspire others with your excitement for life and encourage them to pursue their dreams.

Having **Saturn** in the **First House** makes you come across as a serious and mature person. You're often viewed as reserved, patient, and remarkably wise beyond your years. This might be because you've faced some tough hardships early on, which helped you grow quickly and develop a strong sense of responsibility and self-discipline. Your patience and willingness to wait for the right moments, along with your calm or reserved energy, can be quite noticeable.

You might be a bit more cautious than others when trying new things, and you could be seen as a perfectionist and a dedicated worker. People tend to see you as dependable and grounded. Sometimes self-doubt might visit, and you may be just as critical of yourself as others are, or that's simply the vibe you give off. But with time, you might find it easier to feel comfortable in your own skin and start to respect yourself even more.

You have an alert personality, but as you grow older, you begin to understand the challenges you've endured and the restrictions you've overcome that brought the attentiveness on. This journey helps you appreciate the rewards that come with age and experience.

Uranus in the **First House** makes you unforgettable. There's something about you that stands out, even if you don't try. You may be seen as peculiar, original, eccentric, independent, or unpredictable, and you probably have a love for doing things your own way. This placement gives you a strong desire for freedom and individuality.

Self-expression and authenticity matter to you because you're not afraid of who you are or to show it. You don't mind rules if they make sense, but if they don't, you will break them. People may pick up and feel your rebellious spirit as soon as they meet you. Your style, how you dress, your opinions, or how you approach life may go against the norm, and that's precisely the point and is what makes you stand out.

You're not the type to conform; you question people, everything, and especially authority. Whether it's your appearance, your vibe, or your sudden changes in direction, you're never boring. You are highly intelligent, but just as unusual, and you like that about yourself.

Having **Neptune** in your **First House** gives you a dreamy, glamorous, ethereal presence that can sometimes feel almost inhuman. As a naturally born empath, please be mindful of the company you keep, as you tend to absorb others' energies and might even attract energy vampires. People might project a lot onto you, so setting restrictions is important. Others might find you intriguing, artistic, or even hard to read.

You might have some ocean eyes, light blue or a lighter color, just pure and beautiful. You might be someone with a sensitive soul who enjoys helping those less fortunate. You aren't someone with a big ego; in fact, sometimes you may struggle with how you truly are perceived. You could also have an affinity for changing your appearance, reflecting your adaptable, chameleon-like nature.

This placement boosts your spiritual and creative energies but might also bring some confusion about your identity or lead to an identity crisis at times. You may find boundaries challenging or notice that people project their fantasies onto you. Despite all this, your deep empathy and intuitive softness shine through as you navigate life with kindness and understanding.

With **Pluto** in the **First House**, your presence is authoritative even when you don't say a word. You have an intense energy that others can feel immediately, but most people have a hard time reading you. Others notice there's a depth in you that reflects change, survival, and inner strength. You may have gone through significant shifts in how you see yourself.

Your path might explore themes of death and rebirth, sometimes literally, and often symbolically. People may find you both intimidating and magnetic, leading to strong reactions from others at times. This can be either positive or negative, depending on how they respond to your energy. This placement gives you a private yet commanding presence that reflects the deep intensity of your personal journey. It's a powerful placement and can sometimes be a bit challenging, as it might make it difficult for others to be around you. Don't fret, though, because you are naturally intuitive and gifted.

2nd House: The House of Money & Worth
Ruler: Taurus
First Quadrant (Houses 1-3) Personal Development

The Second House is ruled by Taurus and governed by Venus. While the First House is all about discovering who you are and how you appear to the world, the Second House is where you begin to build your life based on that identity. The Second House is a house of value, money, possessions, self-worth, security, and comfort. It will tell you how you could make your own money. It also speaks about your relationship with resources, how you earn and spend, and what you do to feel balanced and grounded in the physical world. What makes you feel luxurious? This house can tell you how you might enjoy the little things in life.

The Second House remains part of the First Quadrant, keeping its connection to personal development. Here, the focus shifts to perceptions of value, beginning with one's self-worth. Do you feel you are enough? Do you trust your abilities to support yourself? Can you see your talents and find ways to monetize them? The Second House helps clarify these questions.

This space in the chart rules income and material possessions, but it also digs deeper: it shows how you measure your own worth, what you value (emotionally and materially), and how you build a base of security for yourself.

If you have planets in this house, they will influence your outlook on wealth, material stability, and your self-esteem. Not every home will have planets in it. Some are ruled only by a sign, and that is okay.

For example, if Gemini rules your 2nd house, then you are a **Taurus Rising**. Here, your relationship with money and possessions is connected to ideas, communication, intelligence, and a variety of... well, things. You aren't someone who feels satisfied doing the same thing every day to earn a living. You must have mental stimulation in your work and flexibility in how you earn money, or you may even take on multiple jobs at once. Freelancing, writing, blogging, tutoring, social media, podcasting, or anything that would allow you to use your voice or mind will do you well in earning money.

Let's say you are a **Gemini Rising** and have Cancer in the second house. This means that your self-worth is somewhat connected to your home life, your nurturing ability, and your capacity to care for those around you. It also relates to your sense of security and how financially safe you feel. This isn't just a place where home is just a home; it is your foundation. You want it to represent you emotionally, physically, and financially.

You are someone who wants to care for others and make a positive impact. You may work in healthcare, food services, teaching, healing, or find fulfillment in roles like being a stay-at-home mom or simply being a mom. Your financial stability and self-worth can fluctuate like the phases of the Moon. Your work needs to feel meaningful to you to enjoy doing it.

This placement also indicates emotional spending; you might comfort yourself by buying cozy items, food, or things that remind you of home. Budgeting may need to include room for comfort. These individuals make excellent interior designers, cooks, bakers, and childcare workers. They simply desire peace while earning a living.

If you have any planets in your Second House, here's what each of them could mean for you:

When the **Sun** is in your **Second House**, your identity is closely tied to your values, possessions, work, and sense of self-worth. You shine when you feel secure, whether that means through financial stability, emotional grounding, or simply knowing you have something solid to stand on. This is the time when you feel the best. Your confidence increases when your efforts bring visible, tangible rewards, and you often take pride in what you build, own, or provide.

Others may see you as grounded, resourceful, and dependable, someone who values stability and quality in all areas of life. This placement carries a Taurus-like trait, as the Second House is traditionally ruled by Venus, giving you an appreciation for beauty, comfort, physical touch, and the finer things that make life feel safe and abundant. You may feel most alive when surrounded by things you've earned through your own effort, and your sense of identity can be linked to your ability to support yourself and those you love. When finances or stability shake up, you can easily question your own worth, feeling off-balance or insecure, maybe even frustrated and depressed, until you regain your stability.

In astrology, the Sun also represents the father or a father figure, and with it placed here, that relationship often impacts your understanding of worth and security. Maybe he taught you the importance of hard work, self-sufficiency, and creating something lasting, or his example made you determined to build your own sense of stability. Whether his lessons came through guidance or in a challenging approach, they likely shaped your drive to establish a solid foundation and prove you can do it. Just remember, there is more to you than your bank account and how hard you work.

With the **Moon** in your **Second House**, your emotional well-being is linked to how safe, secure, and valued you feel. When life feels steady, and you know your needs are met, your emotions settle; when things feel uncertain, or resources run low, you can feel it deeply and might panic. Money and stability may subside and flow in rhythm with your moods, reflecting how much emotional energy you pour into creating a sense of comfort and belonging. You're likely intuitive about your finances, sometimes spending based on how you feel, or saving and holding tight when you need emotional control.

This placement brings a strong attachment to what feels familiar and comforting. You may have favorite foods, cozy spaces, and sentimental keepsakes that soothe you when the world feels unpredictable. Emotional security often manifests in material things, such as having a warm home, good meals, or the ability to provide for yourself and others. Because the Moon is ever-changing, financial fluctuations or shifts in your possessions can stir up deep feelings, and full moons might even highlight these emotional-material themes more strongly.

In astrology, the Moon symbolizes the mother or maternal figure, and having it in the Second House suggests that your early relationship with her shaped how you relate to comfort, your self-worth, and sense of nourishment. She may have taught you, directly or indirectly, that love is shown through care or the sharing of resources. At times, you might have absorbed her anxieties about money or safety, which can make you extra sensitive to instability later in life. This placement encourages you to nurture yourself the way she may have nurtured you, or the way you wished she had, by creating a life that feels steady and secure, most importantly, emotionally fulfilling.

Having **Mercury** in the **Second House** brings a practical and strategic approach to your resources. You think clearly about values, security, and stability. Your mindset about abundance and your inner conversations can serve as your energetic currency; if you believe you have the money, then it becomes a reality for you. You probably enjoy chatting about money and the way you value things in relationships, and you might find joy in making money through writing, speaking, teaching, or working with technology.

You're often curious about investing and enjoy learning how to make your money grow. Your self-worth might be closely linked to how smart or capable you feel, especially when it comes to managing your finances.

Sometimes, you might overthink your ability to achieve financial security, which can make it tough to separate your self-esteem from your financial mindset. Be aware that with this placement, your finances could see unexpected changes. Perhaps you didn't have much money growing up, and then suddenly you find yourself with a comfortable financial cushion. Conversely, if your financial situation was abundant before, it might unexpectedly diminish.

With **Venus** in the **Second House**, you're drawn to money and comfort more easily than others. It's an excellent placement that blesses you with an eye for beauty, a love of luxury, and a flair for the extravagant. You likely enjoy the finer things in life and have a great sense of style. There's a sweet, sensual touch to how you handle your belongings and how you indulge yourself. You probably look for relationships that mirror your values, and you might feel most loved when you receive something beautiful or physical.

This placement can bring success in fields like beauty, interior design, or entertainment, such as singing, acting, or modeling. Your love language is giving and receiving gifts. It also grants you a natural charm that can help you build wealth or create a lifestyle you truly love. Just remember, don't define your worth only by how polished your life appears on the outside, because true beauty and luxury come from within. With this placement, you might even attract a financially stable partner.

Mars, the malefic planet, here in the **Second House**, means you're a self-starter when it comes to making money and building a life for yourself. You want to earn your worth and will do whatever it takes. This placement gives a strong drive to create stability, but it also means you may face some conflicts around money or self-worth. You likely work best when you're actively pursuing financial or personal goals, and you may get upset when progress is slow, taking forever to reach the result. You fight for what you value and can sometimes come across as defensive if someone questions you about what you bring to the table.

You are not the kind of person to ask others for help because you want to do everything yourself. It is possible that this stems from your childhood, when you felt you had to take on everything on your own without relying on others. You want to manage your own money and not depend on others to feel financially stable. You are great at problem-solving and at creating a space that motivates you to achieve your financial goals. Since you are self-motivated, you absolutely can reach a state of well-being and security. You would do well to own your own business, pursue entrepreneurship, and be your own boss. It's giving head bitch in charge vibes.

When **Jupiter** lands in the **Second House**, there's a natural richness to your finances or the potential to attract it over time. This planet brings the most luck to your life through money and self-worth. You are lucky through investments, specifically in real estate and stocks. Having this placement can help you benefit from certain expenses in your life being taken care of, such as getting a loan forgiven, a car paid for, winning the lottery, or receiving an ample allowance. You really are lucky!

You might be generous with your resources by sharing with others and believe in the power of investing in yourself, or you hold values around progress, education, or travel. You likely feel smitten when you're surrounded by things that represent your ideals. Your self-worth grows the more you embrace your talents and trust that the universe will support you. Focus on developing and continuing self-improvement by learning more about something you're interested in, educating yourself in ways to earn more money, and focusing on your relationship with money. Do this, and you will be on the right track.

Just be conscious not to overspend or assume that good fortune will always last without planning things through. Still, this is one of the more fortunate placements for wealth and self-confidence, especially when things are aligned with your beliefs.

Saturn in the **Second House** can bring a slower, more stable approach to building your resources. You may have faced limitations reflecting on your finances. You likely had to work hard for what you have to feel secure, or you might have struggled to go without at times, whether financially or emotionally. This placement encourages patience as you build your worth step by step.

It's important to note that this is where you develop a deep appreciation for money once you receive it. You might demonstrate strong discipline with your money, either through working hard or saving what

116

you have. You may have a cautious relationship with money, but it gives you the self-control to achieve long-term security if you stay consistent. You take what you own seriously, whether it's through material possessions or your core values. Over time, this placement often leads to deep self-respect, earned through effort.

Neptune in the **Second House** can make your sense of value, your relationship with money, and your self-worth feel vague, hazy, or naïve. You know you are doing all the right things to make money, but you don't feel aligned in your work. You might be overly generous to the point of being a fault or have difficulty seeing your finances clearly. However, on the flip side, you might make money by doing spiritual work through art, healing, or creative activities with your time.

You deeply value empathy and may struggle setting boundaries when others are in need or asking for your help. It is vital to set clear boundaries around spending and earning money here. You may have to come to terms with the fact that you sometimes don't think clearly about your relationship with finances. You are the kind of person who isn't materialistic and prefers to keep your financial situation private; however, you might not manage your money as well as you should.

You may need to work through any illusions about your worth before you feel truly grounded, but once you align your core values with your spiritual truth, this placement can be magical.

Pluto in the **Second House** means that you may have grown up with limited resources. You might have been poor growing up, and that is possible due to the financial hardships you experienced with your parents. There might not have been enough to go around, which could have created a sense of shame around the family's monetary situation. On the other hand, some people have the polar opposite experience: plenty of economic abundance, but parents who withheld those resources in a controlling way.

This contrast can lead to feeling as though you are sacrificing yourself to gain prosperity, giving away some of your power to others in exchange for resources and money. In either case, having Pluto here gives you a powerful lesson about what control and loss truly are, and how to navigate these themes of money and self-worth. Furthermore, your relationship with money will change throughout your life; you will go through periods of having a lot and others when you might not have much. Each time, you come out stronger than before.

For example, there may have been times when you lost everything and had to rebuild from scratch, but there is also a possibility that you can become seriously wealthy and successful. This placement can give you an intense drive to create wealth and security, especially after you have been knocked down. Additionally, you may become involved in power struggles around possession, control, or dependence. Over time, your values grow and change.

While you may hold your values close to your chest, when you own your worth without fear, there is no stopping you. Ultimately, as you continue to renovate your values and self-esteem, you gain both personal empowerment and the ability to foster true prosperity, making each step of your journey meaningful and life-changing.

3rd House: The House of Learning & Communication
Ruler: Gemini
First Quadrant (Houses 1-3) Personal Development

The Third House, ruled by lively Gemini and intelligent Mercury. While the Second House focuses on what you value in life, how you value yourself, and how you build security, the Third House shifts towards how you perceive things and process the world around you. This house encompasses thought, speech, communication, learning styles, and curiosity. It includes your early environment, including siblings, neighbors, and the community you grew up in. It also reflects your style of short-distance travel, both physically and mentally. This house seeks to show how willing you are to new ideas and the way you process them.

This house oversees how you speak, write, think, and network with others, and because of that, it's the part of your chart that rules our conversations, text messages, journaling, and even how you interpret what others say to you. That is where intellect shines at its brightest. It also points to your mindset from childhood and early education, and to how you connected (or didn't) with those who are closest to you and in your immediate surroundings.

This house falls within the First Quadrant; the themes here are still personal, but now we're focusing on how you mentally position yourself in the world. How do you prefer to learn? Do you think before you speak, or just blurt out everything you think, like word vomit? Your third house can help you answer all these questions.

If you have any planets in this house, they shape the way you communicate, learn, and mentally engage in life. If you don't have planets here, the sign ruling your 3rd House still tells a big story.

For example, if Pisces rules your 3rd House, then you are likely a **Capricorn Rising**. With Pisces in the 3rd House, your mind is artistic, intuitive, and often operating in the background like a dream. You may communicate in poetic or symbolic ways, and you're someone who listens, someone who can read between the lines rather than just taking words at face value. You're likely a daydreamer or someone who processes information through feelings and imagery.

School was probably not your favorite place, unless it offered you some emotional or creative freedom. You need softness and empathy in your everyday conversations, and you may have grown up in an environment that requires compassion or that fosters escape affinities. Pisces here can also show psychic or mediumistic tendencies that develop early, especially in sensing the mood of your environment. You are a gentle soul when communicating, but struggle when misunderstood.

Sometimes your thoughts are too much to express clearly. You don't usually like a rigid, strict routine or going down a standard educational path. You learn best when you are allowed to express yourself and think outside the box. You are probably drawn to music, writing, or some form of spiritual communication when describing the world around you.

If you're a **Sagittarius Rising** with Aquarius in your 3rd house, your mind is unique, inquisitive, confident, and you are a bit of a revolutionary speaker. You speak quickly, as if you might be in a hurry. You thrive in fast-paced, stimulating conversations. You say what you mean and mean it loudly, with an intellectual edge that makes you stand out from others. This placement craves constant mental stimulation, movement, or new ideas to stay engaged.

You may have grown up around talkative siblings or neighbors. It's possible you love techy gadgets; sometimes, with this placement, your siblings or neighbors may have pushed you to find your voice. Aquarius ruling the 3rd House gives you unique opinions and a quirky way of expressing them. While your communication style can be quick and sometimes emotionally detached, it's also characterized by honesty and innovation. Your mind craves forming new unconventional paths, and you might get bored easily with traditional standards.

You probably rebelled in your traditional school environments; you might have been the one to stand out in some way. You tend to learn best in interactive, technology-driven environments. As you've grown, you've gravitated toward roles that blend communication and innovation, like debating, public speaking, advocating, writing, or teaching.

If you have any planets in the Third House, here's what each of them might bring to your communication style and learning path.

When the **Sun** is in your **Third House**, your identity is shaped by communication, learning, and your connections with others. You truly shine when you express yourself, share ideas, and interact with those around you. There's a lively curiosity within you, and you tend to notice details that others might overlook. You probably always have something to say or are eager to learn new things, even if it's just to satisfy your own curiosity.

This placement has a lively Gemini-like energy, as the Third House is ruled by Mercury, which gives you a sharp wit, strong social instincts, and a natural talent for self-expression. You feel most alive when you're learning, writing, speaking, or exchanging ideas. You might excel in areas like communication, networking, teaching, or media. Your confidence increases when you feel heard and understood by others.

In astrology, the Sun also symbolizes the father or a father figure, whose influence can shape how you think, communicate, and what you might believe. He might have encouraged your curiosity or love for independent thinking, enjoyed conversations and debates, or always had a story to tell. Sometimes, he may have been inconsistent, busy, or emotionally distant, yet intellectually inspiring. Whatever the case, this relationship has shaped how you voice your opinions and stand up for yourself.

Siblings and cousins can truly enrich your personal growth journey. Whether by offering support or engaging in friendly competition, they encourage you to explore and understand yourself better. As you spend time together, you gradually recognize the value of your own ideas, and sharing them can deepen your connections and boost your confidence. Your innate curiosity and desire to connect are outstanding qualities that can lead to meaningful fulfillment and happiness.

With the **Moon** in your **Third House**, your emotions are deeply connected to how you think, speak, and interpret the world around you. You tend to overthink a lot, and your mind races at 90 mph. You feel most comfortable when you can express what's on your mind and have someone truly listen. Talking things through helps you release emotional tension, especially if you struggle with depression or anxiety, and writing may serve as an outlet when your heart feels heavy.

Your moods can shift rapidly, just like your thoughts do. Usually, your emotional state naturally reflects the atmosphere of your surroundings. You're incredibly intuitive and intelligent, easily sensing the feelings of those around you, sometimes even taking on their moods without meaning to. Because of this sensitivity, it's often helpful to find some quiet or alone time to recharge both your mind and heart. Remember, conversations have the power to lift you up or bring you down, depending on how safe and comfortable you feel sharing your feelings.

Your early environment, whether it was siblings, neighbors, or extended family, played a big role in shaping how you experienced emotions and learned to share your feelings. Perhaps among them were caring figures who took on motherly roles or provided emotional support whenever you needed it.

In astrology, the Moon symbolizes the nurturing mother or maternal figure in your life. When it's positioned this way, her influence might have gently taught you how to express your feelings, or sometimes made you a bit cautious about sharing them. Whether she encouraged you to be open or kept emotional connection reserved, her example likely played a role in shaping how you communicate your truth and how safe you feel doing so. She may have felt like a caring friend throughout your upbringing.

Mercury feels right at home in the **Third House**, which means your mind is constantly active and full of ideas. Here, this planet is in its regular beat, making you a speed-talker who can juggle several mental projects effortlessly. You're naturally curious, quick on your feet, witty, social, and a natural at communicating. Learning is likely something you truly enjoy, and you probably have a sharp memory to match. Journaling, writing, speaking, and talking are all perfect outlets for your energy.

You tend to remember more details than most, and you love adding to your mental library, and sharing that knowledge with others brings you joy. Engaging in idea exchanges and staying mentally stimulated excites you. Your talent for multitasking is sharp, as long as you stay focused and avoid scattering your energy. You might often be the one in your family explaining things to others, acting as the messenger. Also, having Mercury here could mean your siblings are quick-witted and talkative, adding to the lively atmosphere around you.

Venus in your **Third House** suggests that you communicate with warmth and charm, and your words often inspire connection and understanding. You naturally create harmony around you and are seen as a likable, kind, and beautiful person. Sometimes, this may have caused misunderstandings or jealousy from others at school. You also have a wonderful talent for writing or a passion for artistic activities like poetry, storytelling, or other creative pursuits.

Since you enjoy mental stimulation, you'll find great joy in partnering with someone who shares that same curiosity. Most likely, you'll start out as friends with your romantic partners, and you're very intuitive about who your future lovers might be. You probably have a lovely singing voice that adds to your charm. Your conversations mean a lot to you, and because of this, you're naturally drawn to love and connection through exchanging ideas, intellectual chemistry, and heartfelt discussions.

Your siblings or extended family can also have a creative touch when it comes to this placement. Perhaps you grew up in a household filled with sisters or a lot of feminine energy. There's a chance you might have met your partner back in grade school, during a fun short trip, or while expressing your creativity and voice. You could even have met through a sibling, cousin, or neighbor.

Mars in the **Third House** means that your words have a huge impact; people are sure to remember what you say, for better or worse. You aren't someone others enjoy arguing with because you're blunt and can be downright vicious with your words. Your mouth can get you into a lot of trouble; however, you can talk your way out of it. You might find yourself debating or arguing when you're passionate, but you're also incredibly daring when it comes to expressing your ideas.

You would be a great lawyer. You think quickly, are calculating, act on impulse, and may even drive fast, so watch out for road rage! Either way, you're the kind of person who isn't afraid to speak your mind. You stand up for what you believe in and take immediate action when something needs to be said or done, regardless of what others might think. While you may cuss like a sailor, it's often part of your lively charm. You may have had issues with siblings or extended family when Mars is here in the third house.

If you have **Jupiter** in the **Third House**, you might find yourself inherently drawn to storytelling or teaching. You're someone who tends to think creatively and dream big. Your gift for communication is truly special because you're quick-witted, charming, and capable of inspiring others. It's impressive how versatile you are, with talents spanning across media, teaching, writing, production, and public speaking. Remember to embrace and celebrate all these outstanding qualities!

By incorporating these communication skills, you'll find it easier to attract financial abundance and open doors to new opportunities. Your mind enjoys expanding through reading, travel, or philosophy. You're probably someone who loves to read and may inspire others with your journey. Just remember, even your big ideas are most potent when balanced with completing your projects. You might have many siblings by steps, half, or just a large family in general. It's possible that a sibling could be a teacher or educator. Looking back, you probably did well in school and enjoyed traveling, even short trips nearby as a child, which helped shape your adventurous spirit.

When **Saturn** shows up in your **Third House**, it might mean you faced some early hurdles with communication, like feeling shy, experiencing social anxiety, or having a serious mindset. Over time, you'll find yourself improving and gaining confidence in this area. This position can sometimes be linked to learning difficulties, cognitive challenges, anxiety, or depression. Remember, your words matter, whether you're careful to think before you speak or prefer to stay quiet to avoid conflicts.

You're probably a thoughtful and focused person, possibly with excellent teaching or writing skills. When it comes to relationships with siblings or extended family, Saturn here can bring a sense of responsibility and serious interactions. Sometimes, this might create some distance, feelings of obligation, or a need to set clear boundaries. Remember, this placement can teach you valuable lessons in patience and compromise with your siblings. It encourages understanding and finding common ground. It doesn't mean you lack love; instead, it focuses on some challenges you might face together.

You can also improve your communication skills by focusing on structure and discipline. Building relationships with your peers and those around you might be challenging at first due to communication difficulties, making it feel hard to connect. However, with time, you can overcome these obstacles, and those who get to know you will see how witty and funny you truly are. This journey is also a fantastic opportunity to pursue a career as a therapist or counselor, as you develop a deep understanding of listening and conversation and effortlessly offer thoughtful advice and attentive listening.

Uranus in the **Third House** proposes that your mind naturally jumps between quick bursts of thought and unpredictable routes. Your way of communicating tends to be refreshingly quirky, inventive, or even genius-level. Technology is a close companion for you. While your thoughts are often ahead of their time, taking some time to stay grounded can help harness your full mental potential.

You might have gone through some unexpected changes in your early education, like moving from public school to homeschooling, or maybe you were the adventurous type who got into trouble and was expelled. Perhaps you experienced frequent moves or traveled to various places as a child. You might notice moments of sudden insight that seem to come out of nowhere, and you're often drawn to one-off topics, innovative learning methods, or even futuristic ideas. Your communication style can be sharp, witty, or a bit eccentric, and valuing intellectual freedom might be very important to you. Ultimately, you cherish the ability to think independently and forge your own path.

When thinking about siblings or extended family, these relationships can sometimes shift unexpectedly, creating moments of distance or a strong sense of individuality. Perhaps you have a sibling who is quite different, rebellious, or very independent, or maybe you've sometimes felt like the black sheep in your family, forging your own unique path from an early age. It's also possible that you grew up as an only child.

Having **Neptune** in the **Third House** blends your sense of logic and intuition. You probably had a hard time focusing on school when you were a kid, maybe due to ADHD or just a naturally wandering attention span. Your dreamy nature makes you a creative and empathetic soul, often receiving heartfelt messages from loved ones in dreams. Your unique way of communicating can sometimes seem a bit mysterious or hard to follow, but that only makes your character all the more charming and intriguing.

Your imagination is truly inspiring and can whisk you away to any place you dream of. When it comes to siblings or extended family, Neptune here might bring some funny misunderstandings or just a touch of impracticality. You might share a deep emotional or spiritual connection with your siblings, sometimes feeling like their needs and feelings are a bit tricky to fully grasp. Your relationships with extended family are often caring and filled with empathy and compassion, though, of course, misunderstandings or blurred boundaries can sometimes happen.

Neptune in the third house gently suggests that your family could have influenced your imagination or spirituality. You might have embraced roles like being the peacemaker or the dreamer in your family. Just a friendly reminder to be mindful of your words, as what you think often finds its way into what you say.

Having **Pluto** in the **Third House** means that you're an extremely intuitive and intense person. You enjoy exploring questions and seeking answers until everything makes sense because your curiosity is driven by a desire to uncover life's mysteries. Sometimes, you might seem a bit intimidating because you're very perceptive, picking up on what others are saying and feeling. Your words and thoughts often carry a mysterious and powerful tone. With your sharp mind, you also have a keen and expressive way of communicating.

You love exploring and chatting about rare topics, including taboo subjects like witchcraft, astrology, tarot, and palmistry. This placement of Pluto hints that you might have faced some struggles with authority involving your siblings or experienced control issues in your early environment, with kids at school, with neighbors, or within your extended family. During early childhood, you may have learned what it feels like to be powerless through these experiences. As a result, you might sometimes face mental health challenges, learning difficulties, or even behavioral issues. Your path is about discovering life's truths, and you might be naturally drawn to psychology, investigation, or deep, meaningful conversations that get to the heart of things.

Having siblings or extended family can sometimes create tough dynamics. Maybe you've experienced relationships filled with issues of control, secrets, or deep emotional struggles that helped you grow stronger and more resilient. You might have had to work through complicated family situations or even become a catalyst for positive change in your family. As a child, you may have felt isolated and had to keep secrets, maybe ones for others, too. Your psychic insights are very sharp and, at times, can even feel overwhelming, even for you. It's so important to share your story and let others hear you, allow yourself to be seen and understood. Honestly, it's about time! I truly encourage you to consider writing a book about your life.

4th House: The House of Home & Roots
Ruler: Cancer
Second Quadrant (Houses 4–6): Personal Relationships & Immediate Environment

Cancer and the Moon rule the Fourth House. It marks the base of the birth chart, known in Latin as the "bottom of the sky" or the IC (Imum Coeli). This house represents your roots and your private world. It is your home and the emotional foundation on which the rest of your chart is built. Here is the realm of your ancestors, your family lineage, and your relationship with your parents (especially the one who nurtured you most). The Fourth House holds the emotional imprint left by your early environment in this world.

Previously, we looked at how the First Quadrant (Houses 1–3) influences your sense of identity and how you see yourself. Now, let's explore the Second Quadrant, which focuses on your relationships and the environments that support or challenge you. The Fourth House functions as the base of your upbringing, grounding your sense of home, your roots, both the ones you come from and the ones you're building now for the future.

This house symbolizes your family of origin, ancestral karma, private life, and the memories and emotional habits you formed during your earliest years on earth. It speaks to the legacy you inherited from your parents, especially from whoever nurtured you most. It carries the emotional tone of your upbringing, your connection to home, and your need for safety and belonging. This is where your core wounds and comforts live and breathe, and where you go to retreat, restore, and ground yourself.

The Fourth House represents your physical surroundings, like your home and land. It's where your connection to real estate, your aim to own property, and your deep roots come into focus. This house also shows how your family and heritage have helped shape your innermost self, guiding how you nurture others and support your family tree. Think of it as the heart of your chart, your special space. Remember, planets in this house influence how you connect with your home, family, comfort, and emotional security. Even if no planets are present, the sign that rules your 4th House still offers meaningful insights into these areas story.

For example, if Leo rules your 4th House, you might be a **Taurus Rising**. When Leo influences this area, your home often feels like a special sanctuary full of pride, where you love to showcase your creativity and radiate warmth to everyone around. Bright, bold colors in your decor could mirror your lively personality.

Your internal world longs to be recognized and cherished by those close to you. Sometimes, affection might have felt conditional, perhaps because you grew up in a household where you had to perform or where appearances mattered a lot. The living room may have been your stage for entertaining. Maybe a parent was very dominant, or your parents were bubbly and outgoing. If you were the "gifted one" in the family, you might have felt the pressure to meet high expectations.

Your parents likely saw your potential and nurtured your talents, but depending on other aspects related to this house, it could have been the opposite, where you felt overlooked, unsupported, or even rejected and bullied.

As an adult, you now want your home to reflect your unique self. You love being in spaces that are expressive, inspiring, and full of love. Loyalty is especially important to you because your emotional safety depends on the trustworthiness and devotion of those around you. You seek a home where you feel truly safe. This placement might inspire you to take on a leadership role within your family, reflecting your natural desire to protect and lead.

If Capricorn rules your 4th House, you're probably a **Libra Rising**. Your early home life might have felt strict, sometimes tumultuous, stressful, and very traditional when it came to family values and relationships. You may have had to grow up quickly because your parents couldn't always meet your needs. Sometimes you had to be independent or carry the emotional weight of those around you.

It's possible you took on a job in your early years to help out at home and faced some financial constraints. Your caregivers might have been busy, stubborn, stern, or emotionally distant at times. This placement of Saturn often creates a strong internal desire for control and stability at home. You feel safest when your environment feels reliable and steady.

As an adult, your home becomes your sanctuary. You probably like a space that's efficient, cozy, and not cluttered. While opening up emotionally at home might not come naturally, underneath your calm exterior is a bottomless well of inner strength and loyalty. You're here to break free from your inherited emotional patterns, reshaping your foundation, and creating a lasting safe space and resilience around you, something very different from your early experiences.

If you have any planets in the Fourth House, they bring even more energy into your emotional world, your family life, and your connection to home.

If you have the **Sun** in the **Fourth House**, your personality is intensely private, but when you feel comfortable being yourself, you become radiant and open. Your identity is closely connected to your roots, home, creativity, and the emotional foundation that shaped you into who you are today. You could be a stay-at-home mom or dad, or even be the rock of the family. This placement gives you Cancer-like qualities, since the Fourth House is traditionally ruled by the Moon, making you attuned to family bonds, memories, and what feels familiar.

You come across as such a warm and caring person, especially when you feel safe and supported by trusted loved ones and are in comforting spaces. Your close family and friends see you as a steadfast anchor, and others are naturally drawn to your kind presence. Your family plays a special role in building your confidence because you can gauge how they perceive you, whether through their encouragement or the acknowledgment you work so hard for. There is a deep sense of pride in your heritage and in the rich emotional legacy passed down through generations, a birthright you cherish.

Your home truly reflects who you are, serving as a sanctuary where you can relax and find your peace. You naturally have a caring heart, often looking after loved ones with warmth and kindness. In astrology, the Sun also symbolizes the father or a father figure, influencing your emotional foundation in momentous ways. Sometimes, your father might have been both a provider and a nurturer, or perhaps your mother stepped into roles usually linked to a father; maybe your father was absent or unknown. Regardless of which parent played that influential role, their presence or absence greatly shaped your understanding of love, security, and belonging to something.

Having the **Moon** in the **Fourth House** places it in her natural domain, creating a very powerful position. You tend to keep your emotions close, preferring not to cry in public and usually sharing your feelings only with those you trust most or when you're alone. Since the Moon rules Cancer, and Cancer governs the 4th house, early family experiences can have a deep influence on your feelings and emotional state. This placement often brings to my mind the warmth and closeness of Lorelai and Rory (Gilmore Girls reference), especially if well-aspected, getting along well with your mom, and a bond that feels more like friendship.

However, if the aspects aren't so favorable, it could mean that you felt like your role was more like that of a parent, or you experienced emotional disconnection from your parents or a parent. Family, especially on your mother's side, likely has a significant impact on your emotions. You may have been very sensitive as a child, carrying that tenderness into adulthood. To you, home is everything: it's not just a physical space, but an emotional sanctuary that makes you feel complete. You find comfort in being at home, in your own space.

This is a cozy Moon placement; you love creating a warm, safe atmosphere. You often feel nostalgic, missing the comfort of home or wishing for what family could have been. You may have had a close, nurturing bond with your mother or a maternal figure who provided support and guidance.

In astrology, the Moon represents the mother or a maternal figure. She might have been a source of reassurance, guidance, or stability, shaping how you nurture yourself and others. Sometimes this placement suggests that your mother took on a central role in the household. Because of that, you might try to recreate that sense of comfort in your own home. You feel most secure when your emotional needs are fulfilled at home, and you likely need time alone to reflect and manage your feelings.

You have a natural intuition for understanding what those around you need emotionally. You probably have a good sense of reading the room and knowing what family members or loved ones are feeling.

Having **Mercury** in the **Fourth House** shows that you process your thoughts quietly and privately. You might feel a strong connection to your home life, emotions, and memories. Your childhood could have been lively, filled with conversations, meaningful moments with family, or even lots of moving around. Perhaps your home was a cozy place full of books, where writing played a special part in life, maybe even for a parent. Education likely meant a lot to your family, and you may have been encouraged to stay on top of your schoolwork, possibly even being homeschooled at some point.

Your home life is vibrant and filled with chatter. Your family is a talkative bunch, and they are quick as a whip, too! You might often have been the one translating for your family or helping to organize their thoughts and plans. Sometimes, you find absolute joy in reflecting on your past, whether it's through journaling, exploring your family history, or writing about your own childhood. You tend to express your feelings by talking them out, and your home is a place where your mind feels the most comfortable wandering and learning.

Venus in the **Fourth House** suggests that home is where you see beauty and where you express this energy most. You probably grew up in a charming or harmonious household. If not, you longed for it, often dreaming of having your own space to inspire. You might love decorating your home in fine detail.

You enjoy entertaining guests and creating cozy, love-filled environments. You're likely very emotionally close to your family, very protective of them, especially your mother, if this is well aspected, and you are gentle with your family. You find peace at home and with your loved ones. Others feel the warmth you create within your house. You tend to craft emotionally safe and visually appealing spaces. A loving home life is essential for your well-being. Watching the relationships around you as you grow up shapes how you form relationships. It's possible that you could meet your partner at home, near your home, or from someone in your family, maybe they are even a family friend.

Mars in the **Fourth House** tells us you put immense energy into your home. Here's why: Growing up, your home life may have been active, aggressive, or even filled with conflict. You might have had a strict mother who was spiteful or a father who also took on that role, or there may have been arguments, verbal attacks, and even physical assaults from your parents because of their strong personalities. You possibly felt a constant need to defend or assert yourself. Your parents likely fought frequently as well.

It's possible you moved often, or there was always stress in your immediate home environment, possibly because of your parents' destructive behavior. Today, you might be very protective of your space or feel compelled to "fight" for your family. As an adult, you want your

140

home to be a place of action: you need to move, fix, or take control because that's what you learned growing up. It isn't necessarily a place to relax; you are either busy with something or constantly having people come and go. You may feel tension with family members or feel compelled to channel your emotions into physical tasks at home. Be cautious of impulsive reactions in your personal life.

If you have **Jupiter** in the **Fourth House**, it proposes you may have grown up in a lively household rich in cultural diversity. Your family could have been quite unique, possibly including foster siblings, stepsiblings, half-siblings, or even multiple parents. Maybe you weren't raised by your biological parents at times, living in a big, blended family. It's also possible that you traveled frequently as a child or moved around often.

Although your family relationships might not be very close due to differing beliefs and values, you may have a special spiritual or religious practice that is very personal to you, shared only with close friends, or kept private. Your family might have served as teachers, guides, helpers, or storytellers, offering wisdom, encouraging kindness, or helping you learn important life lessons. You could find luck and positive energy through your family, your home, or even the physical house itself. Just be mindful of potential hoarding tendencies with this placement.

You probably have a keen mind and a strong faith, especially when it comes to family matters and emotional healing. You might feel truly fulfilled when your home life expands through travel, discovery of new cultures, or even the building of a large family of your own. Jupiter in the

141

4th house is considered a fortunate placement, often bringing protection and good luck related to family or real estate later in life.

Having **Saturn** in the **Fourth House** could mean that your early home life was quite challenging, especially in your younger years. It could have been a very organized and disciplined environment, but also one filled with tension. If your parents had separated, you might have had to move between their households, which could have deeply affected you. You probably took on adult responsibilities early on, which meant you didn't have much time to enjoy the carefree innocence of childhood; you had to grow up fast.

Family members might have seemed distant or cold to you, possibly because they felt overwhelmed by their own responsibilities, and this burden was often pushed onto you. You may have experienced a strained relationship with your mother, missed emotional nurturing, or not spent as much time with her as you wished. Sometimes, you might have had to look after others or hide your feelings to get through your childhood. Being home could have felt more like a duty than a place of peace and comfort.

As an adult, you likely crave stability and a sense of control over your living space. You might feel freer and more playful now than you did as a child. You're building a meaningful legacy, and you probably take your emotional commitments seriously rather than brushing them aside. It could have been hard for you to feel truly at home until later in life, especially if your upbringing was strict and structured. But once you find that sense of belonging, your inner foundation becomes incredibly strong and unshakeable.

Uranus in the **Fourth House** points to a childhood that may have been unconventional, filled with unique experiences and a sense of independence. You might have moved around a lot or been part of a blended family, raised by a single parent, or by parents who encouraged you to be yourself from a young age. This could have made your early years feel a bit unpredictable. You may sometimes feel like the black sheep of your family, feeling different from others, and valuing your personal freedom and beliefs more than emotional closeness.

As you grow into adulthood, you might find yourself wanting to carve out your own path, sometimes stepping back when things get emotionally intense. This sense of independence can lead to deep reflections on your identity and inspire you to create a home life that truly reflects who you are. You may also prefer living alone, have a bachelor-like tendency, or a home that shows off your unique personality, possibly filled with tech gadgets or quirky decor. Though you enjoy your own company, you also cherish moments with friends, and your childhood experiences have shaped you into someone who grew up differently from other people, giving you a unique perspective on family dynamics.

Neptune in the **Fourth House** paints a picture of a childhood that might have included moments of neglect, abuse, or traumatic events involving a parent or family member. For you, home was more than just a physical space; it was a spiritual sanctuary where you felt safe to dream and express your creativity. With this placement, one or both of your parents could have been deeply intuitive, spiritual, or even artistic. During these early years, you were often developing your artistic talents and creative abilities. Your surroundings often carried an air of emotional depth and a hint of mysticism.

At the same time, Neptune's influence can sometimes bring confusion and unclear boundaries. This might mean that struggles with addiction, escapism, or emotional unavailability played a part in your upbringing, possibly linked to your parents. You may have felt emotionally entangled with a parent or idealized your family life, seeing it through rosy glasses even when things weren't always stable or clear. This placement often creates a deep desire for emotional safety and understanding. As you grow older, you might feel drawn to building a home that feels peaceful, magical, and spiritually secure. Your intuition is closely tied to your family roots, and you may inherit your intuitive gifts from your family members and ancestors.

If **Pluto** is in your **Fourth House**, it shows that your emotions are strongly connected to your family, home life, and feelings of security. Your childhood might have been quite intense, possibly filled with ups and downs, secrets your parents kept, or even some emotional scars. You might have sensed things unfolding beneath the surface that others didn't notice, like recurring family patterns that repeat across generations, affecting everyone.

As you grow older, you probably long for a home where you can freely express your feelings, no matter what. You've likely learned to stay quiet in difficult moments and now refuse to do so as an adult. Early experiences may have taught you how to protect yourself from overwhelming emotions or trauma. Today, your home is a special place, holding peaceful energy and solitude for you. You might feel called to explore ancestral healing, shadow work, or rebuild your emotional foundation from the ground up. With this placement, you hold the potential to transform your family history and create a new path forward.

5th House: The House of Pleasure & Self-Expression

Ruler: Leo

Second Quadrant (Houses 4–6): Personal Relationships & Immediate Environment

The Fifth House is all about how your creativity, romance, and joy blossom in your life! It reflects that wonderful part of you that loves to be seen and appreciated by others. In this area, you're free to express yourself creatively, whatever form that takes. This is the house of happiness, passion, and artistic expression, where you leave a personal legacy through what you create. Whether you're painting, writing poetry, or even nurturing a child, this is the space where your light shines the brightest!

Leo and the Sun naturally energize the Fifth House, encouraging you to nurture what makes you happy, boost your creativity, and enjoy your romantic life and sense of fun. It's a special place where you can genuinely share yourself and find fulfillment. Plus, it reflects your inner child and the part of you that loves the freedom to create without judgment. Here, you can proudly share your talents, dreams, and passions.

While the Fourth House grounds your emotional roots and deep sense of home, the Fifth House builds on those roots by showing how you shine and grow from those roots since your childhood and into your own family you make. It's where true love and individuality come together, creating joy and excitement in your life. Whether that's through art, relationships, or even parenthood, this house reveals what you're proud of, what you love, and where you find that pure happiness in being yourself.

This house is all about your dating life, flings, fertility, and those lively, energetic moments that make life exciting. It's not necessarily about drama in a negative way, but rather the kind that sparks passion and adds a bit of flair. Imagine a life full of passion and performance, where a little playfulness and the occasional chaos can keep things interesting when things feel out of balance. The Fifth House also symbolizes our children, whether physically or symbolically, whether they're here or not. If you're shaping or nurturing something new, you'll see it reflected here. It's all about how we love, create, and bring joy into our lives.

If you have planets in this house, they greatly influence how you express yourself creatively and how you fall in love. If you don't have planets here, the sign on your 5th House still tells an amusing story, and don't worry, not all houses have planets. That's okay. It doesn't mean you'll never experience love or have children; it just means your story emphasizes other parts of your life more. Still, this house remains essential, and everyone has one.

For example, if Virgo influences your 5th House, you might have a **Taurus Rising**. With Virgo here, your creative side tends to be refined, detail-oriented, and often subtly expressed. You might enjoy hobbies like crafting, writing, organizing, or helping others. These activities bring you genuine joy and help you feel grounded.

In love, you may show care through helpful actions rather than grand gestures. When it comes to romance, you're quite selective, valuing deep and meaningful connections over fleeting, spontaneous flings. You enjoy playful activities that have purpose and significance. You prefer to make sure you have quality time for fun, rather than just going with the flow. Your dating life is likely very maintained, and you may have children who naturally care for others and stay organized. They probably enjoy cleanliness and looking well-put-together.

If Aquarius rules your Fifth House, you are likely a **Libra Rising**. With Aquarius in this house of pleasure and self-expression, your creativity tends to be unique, mentally stimulating, and often ahead of its time. You're someone who expresses yourself through originality, whether it's in the way you dress, the art you create, or the unconventional ideas you support. Your hobbies might include tech, astrology, activism, or anything that encourages you to think outside the box or connect with like-minded communities.

When it comes to romance, you're attracted to people who are open-minded, intelligent, and a bit unconventional in how your relationships can unfold. You may not enjoy overly traditional or clingy relationships, preferring partnerships that offer room for freedom and growth. You enjoy experiences that challenge the norm or stimulate your mind. Even when having fun, you crave meaning. Regarding children, if you choose to have them, they may be independent, curious, and socially aware. They might express themselves in nontraditional ways, and you're likely to encourage them to be true to themselves rather than conform to a mold like several others do. These are the kids who think big, asks penetrating questions, and aren't afraid to stand out.

If your **Sun** is in the **Fifth House**, your identity is connected to your self-expression and your playful, inner child. Your personality shines through creative pursuits, filling your life with joy and attracting admiration. You thrive in environments where you can showcase your talents and have fun, giving off a natural performer vibe that effortlessly draws attention. You tend to have lively energy and might enjoy being the life of the party.

This placement strongly reflects Leo characteristics since the Sun rules the Fifth House, lending you a vibrant, playful, and magnetic presence. You feel most like yourself when you're creating, laughing, taking risks, or engaging in romantic pursuits and activities that nurture your inner child. To you, life is to be enjoyed, and you approach this with heartfelt enthusiasm. You likely have a flair for drama, art, performance, entrepreneurship, or pursuits that highlight your unique spark, but you may not appreciate criticism from others.

Recognition means a lot to you; it boosts your confidence. You might also have a special love for children, or you find joy in mentoring and inspiring young people. Speaking of youth, you probably have creative children who love being in the spotlight, too.

In astrology, the Sun often symbolizes the father or a father figure. With this placement, your father may have been fun-loving and supportive of your creative talents or encouraged you to express your identity, possibly making you charismatic, proud, or achievement-oriented if this aligns well with your chart. If not, you might sometimes struggle with self-confidence and motivation to enjoy life fully, and could have a complex relationship with your father. Whether your dad nurtured your confidence or pushed you to seek applause, you naturally carry a positive outlook on life and a zest for living.

Having the **Moon** in the **Fifth House** means that your emotions are beautifully connected to creativity, joy, love, and self-expression. You feel most alive when you're having fun or allowing your inner child to play freely. Your heart is deeply engaged in romance, affection, and those magical moments that make life special. People with this placement often find a wonderful outlet for their feelings through art, performance, or storytelling.

Your mood can change with your experiences in love or when your creative flow is blocked, which might make you feel childish or dramatic at times. You have a natural intuition with children, and they often sense it as well, whether you are nurturing your own or embracing the inner child within yourself and others. You form these emotional bonds through your creative activities, and feeling appreciated and encouraged helps you feel secure, as being seen and valued makes a big difference. When you're around trusted people, you're often openly emotional, which others find warm and endearing.

In astrology, the Moon represents the mother, who may have nurtured your talents or celebrated your uniqueness. Sometimes, she sought the spotlight herself or encouraged you to shine in ways that felt both supportive and a little bit pressured. In some cases, she enjoyed parties, having fun, or the thrill of doing something extreme.

Having **Mercury** in the **Fifth House** reveals a wonderfully artistic and creative spirit that really shines. Your playful and expressive way of communicating adds a beautiful touch to how you share your creativity. You might find yourself naturally drawn to writing, performing, or teaching, and you're likely great at storytelling and visualizing ideas. Chances are, you enjoy acting, singing, speaking, or comedy, and you thrive in connecting with others through these lively, artistic exchanges.

Flirting, witty banter, or clever stories probably come to you with ease. You might also be someone who thoughtfully considers love, children, or the creative journey itself. This could mean your children are also very communicative, quick thinkers, curious travelers, and eager for mental adventures. They love to explore, learn, and happily share their ideas.

Venus in the **Fifth House** reveals a genuinely charming, joyful, and approachable personality that naturally draws others in. You carry a lovely romantic spirit, are drawn to beauty, pleasure, and the act of love simply because they bring you happiness. This placement peaks in on your appreciation for aesthetics, romance, and artistic expression. You're a natural performer, often showcasing your talents with confidence in your creativity and artistic flair. You might be very affectionate and flirtatious, or simply enjoy activities that make you happy. You actually recognize your worth and the positive impact you have! Venus here amplifies your love for beauty and might even inspire you to have creatively gifted, artistic children. If this placement is well-aspected in your chart, you love them enormously, too.

Your style and charm create a captivating, magnetic presence, and having Venus here might mean you meet your partner in fun settings like a concert, a bar, a club, when you're with friends or children, or while engaging in creative hobbies. They are likely to be beautiful, talented, fun, and enjoy showing you off.

Mars in the **Fifth House** suggests that you are a fun person, likely the life of the party. Your passion drives your creativity, creating a yin-and-yang of creative motivation. You pursue love and pleasure boldly and intensely, which may sometimes make you appear quite strong in relationships. You are enthusiastic about many things, but when you're upset, you can be overdramatic.

There may be a competitive streak when it comes to attracting romantic partners' attention or achieving artistic success. You radiate a seductive energy that others notice. You might take risks in romance, pursue lovers passionately, or dive into hobbies with full force. Sometimes, this placement can lead to impulsive behavior in dating or dramatic love stories.

You invest a lot of energy in being a good parent, wanting the best for your children, but this can sometimes come across as controlling. Be sure to consider your partner's and children's interests, rather than focusing only on your own. Your children may be athletic, into adrenaline-filled activities, join the military, or do something related to the body. They may seem impulsive and could be very hard on themselves.

Jupiter in the **Fifth House** signifies abundance through self-expression and the sharing of your creative talents. You have a vibrant personality: outgoing, cheerful, charismatic, driven, bold, and full of fun. Naturally, you draw attention, and because of that, wonderful opportunities often come your way with ease. You're especially lucky when it comes to love or exploring your creative passions. Traveling and seeing the world might be especially fortunate for you, perhaps just for the joy of discovery. People with this placement often have big dreams that others might see as impossible, but you pursue them with enthusiasm.

You make it your life's goal to live fully and joyfully. You might be someone who creates simply for the love of learning or spiritual growth, and you likely have many hobbies. This placement could also indicate a strong bond with children, or even the possibility of a large family; maybe you'll have many kids, adopt, or be the neighborhood mom, but in some way, they bring you happiness and good fortune! You may carry a youthful optimism or faith and enjoy heartfelt conversations with friends about philosophy or your beliefs.

Saturn in the **Fifth House** can make finding happiness feel more challenging early on. You might have believed that whenever you tried to have fun, express yourself, or build confidence, something or someone would take it away. As a result, you may feel like you're not supposed to have fun or that fun isn't meant for adults, leading to worries about what happiness and joy should really look like. You might tend to play it safe, afraid of making mistakes. Even if you want to have fun, you might not know how, which can lead to comparing your life to others.

Maybe you've been shy about sharing yourself with others or felt pressured to "do it right" creatively or romantically. You could look for your self-worth through your romantic relationships. Sometimes growing up too fast means you suppress your playful, childlike side and take everything very seriously. You might feel like childhood was taken from you, or you might experience similar feelings about creating your own children later in life. Having children can be a challenge, or if you do, your relationship with them might be a little strained. Your kids might learn things at their own pace: walking, talking, weaning off the pacifier, or acquiring new skills. They might be late bloomers in some ways, but they often have a wise, old soul and may show maturity or take life seriously earlier than most.

Uranus in the **Fifth House** infuses your creative expression with a unique energy. You might rebel against traditional romantic roles, preferring a partner who enjoys unusual sexual dynamics, or you could pursue unconventional hobbies. Still, you have a clear creative path. Your love life may experience many twists and turns, drawn to people who are open-minded and aren't afraid to be different.

You may find it challenging to commit unless you feel completely free to be yourself and are sure that others accept your eccentric side. Children or creative projects could enter your life suddenly or unexpectedly, such as through an unplanned pregnancy. Regarding children, yours may be a bit unconventional, or your parenting style might be different. You might be the type of parent who is comfortable with your children speaking their minds or pursuing independence earlier than most parents would.

Neptune in the **Fifth House** gives this area a dreamy, romantic, and sometimes cloudy quality. You might idealize love and your partners, or dedicate yourself only to your art. You are likely to put your partners on a pedestal. There is a longing for spiritual and emotional connection in romance, but setting boundaries is crucial. You may be drawn to fantasy, film, or music; whatever it is, it screams multiple creative talents because you are naturally artistic. This placement can foster great creativity, but can also lead to illusions about love.

Be mindful of idealizing what isn't real. You're likely a romantic at heart, longing to be swept away, but it's important to stay aware and establish healthy boundaries. Children connected to this placement may also be imaginative, dreamy, and closely linked to past-life realms. Your children are likely very artistic and intuitive, but sometimes you might feel overwhelmed by parenting and need to escape. Neptune can also promote addictive tendencies, so watch out for addiction to gambling, sex, drugs, or partying, and be aware of how this energy might influence how your children develop.

Pluto in the **Fifth House** intensifies your love life, inner happiness, and creative spirit. It's a house of transformation where you'll experience some of the most exciting changes. Growing up, you might have heard you needed to be a certain way to earn love, and some with this placement could have faced oversexualization at a young age. As you grow, this might show up as power struggles, obsession, overindulgence in physical pleasures, or a tendency to go all-in or not at all in love.

You have a natural desire to find creative ways to express yourself and heal past wounds. Your creative pursuits could lead to soulful connections, helping your inner child heal from emotional scars and inspiring new beginnings. Your children might also have a strong, intense outlook. They could be highly creative, focused on understanding the deeper truths, being direct, wanting the truth upfront, though there might be some secrets either about the children or kept from them in the home.

6th House: The House of Work, Health & Daily Habits

Ruler: Virgo
Second Quadrant (Houses 4–6): Personal Relationships & Immediate Environment

The 6th house is where you get in touch with the real world through your daily routine. It's all about responsibility, helping others, and what your everyday life looks like. This house reflects how you work, handle stress, and take care of your body. Think of it as a focus on self-improvement and your connection to health. Interestingly, it even hints at what kind of pets you might have (or not have) had over time.

The 6th house marks a complete shift from where it's all about fun and play to a more serious area of life where we handle daily tasks, serve others, structure our lives, and practice self-discipline. So, when you think about this area, I want you to ask yourself, how do you take care of your body? How do you approach your work? What is your relationship with routines and even your pets? This house shows how you find purpose in the small daily acts that support a functional life.

If **Leo** is your **Rising** Sign, Capricorn probably influences your 6th House, bringing a warm and practical vibe to how you tackle your daily life. You're naturally disciplined and goal-focused, appreciating structure and order to keep chaos at bay. Routines that support long-term success feel right to you because they add purpose to your everyday moments. It's helpful to set small, achievable goals so you feel like you accomplished something by the end of the day.

You can be highly productive; however, it's important to schedule breaks to prevent burnout. When it comes to health, you're dedicated and take your responsibilities seriously. You thrive when you're making progress or working toward mastery. If you have pets, you might prefer animals that are easy to care for, well-trained, and serve a practical purpose. Having pets also brings a gentle sense of loyalty and companionship into your life, which means a lot to you.

Having your **Sun** in the **Sixth House** suggests your sense of identity is tied to your work and daily rhythms. You find true fulfillment in serving other people, and you appreciate being recognized and valued for your dedication and consistency. This placement highlights Virgo traits that shine through.

You thrive when you feel helpful and appreciated for your efforts. Your most genuine self emerges when you're engaged in productive activities and relaxing can sometimes be a challenge for you. You're likely proud of your work ethic and how you handle responsibilities, often preferring leadership roles in service-related fields.

Your health often emulates your work-life balance, so it's important to watch out for overdoing it, which can lead to burnout. Many people with this placement see pets as part of their family, taking pride in caring for their well-being.

In astrology, the Sun often relates to a father or father figure. In the Sixth House, this might mean your father was quite judgmental or critical about your lifestyle, possibly a perfectionist who wanted the same in you. As a result, you may have felt the need to live in a certain way to gain his approval.

The **Moon** in the **Sixth House** shows how your emotional well-being is linked to your daily routines, work, and environment. Your moods can influence your everyday life, sometimes bringing on feelings of anxiety, especially if routines aren't feeling supportive. It's common for stress to show up in digestion or physical symptoms. To help you feel more balanced, try routines like journaling, meditating, or preparing nourishing meals.

Remember to set aside some time each day just for yourself, as you might tend to overextend. Your natural intuition makes you attentive to the needs of others, often leading you toward caregiving or service roles such as nursing, caregiving, holistic therapy, or working in hospitality, including restaurants. You might also have a special connection with animals. Sometimes, you may naturally take on a nurturing role, such as being a stay-at-home parent. You may also have a strong bond with your pets by finding comfort in their presence.

In astrology, the Moon symbolizes the mother, and for you, she might have been someone with whom you didn't always feel secure. She may have made you believe that to receive love and support, you had to be perfect or constantly doing better.

Having **Mercury** in the **Sixth House** means you have a quick wit and a sharp mind. You might tend to overthink because of perfectionist tendencies, but your thinking is always methodical, logical, and precise. You love structure, routine, and mental engagement in your daily life. Staying busy is enjoyable for you, though it's natural to sometimes feel overwhelmed or experience ADHD or ADD, many of us do these days, especially since life can be draining.

You might even find yourself communicating in rhythm or rhyme as a fun way to complete your tasks! You're likely interested in writing, teaching, or any work that involves communication or attention to detail. You're great at multitasking and staying organized. Just be mindful of overthinking or stress-related issues like anxiety. You're a talented speaker, but sometimes you might hold back because you're your own harshest critic. With Mercury here, you may form really engaging and stimulating bonds with pets, especially those that are smart, playful, and quirky, which keeps your mind lively and your routine enjoyable.

Having **Venus** in the **Sixth House** adds a lovely sense of elegance and a heartfelt desire for harmony to your daily routines, what work is like for you, and your daily surroundings. You find absolute comfort in sensory pleasures, so having a daily self-care routine, yoga, meditation, and skin care, for example, are all excellent for you. You probably enjoy working in cozy, beautiful, peaceful, and eye-pleasing spaces. You may love working in roles related to beauty, wellness, or service, such as in the arts, fashion, health, or hospitality.

Building meaningful relationships with coworkers or those you meet regularly can be very rewarding, and there's a good chance that love might bloom through your work, during your routines, or at your favorite hangout spots. You genuinely appreciate thoughtfulness and small acts of kindness, often sharing and receiving love through caring gestures and acts of service. Cooking for loved ones, planning special outings, and organizing get-togethers bring you joy. Sometimes, you might indulge in comfort or put things off, so finding a healthy balance is key to your overall happiness.

When it comes to pets, you likely treat them as your best friends, spoiling them rotten with affection and choosing animals that reflect your sense of beauty and warmth. Growing up, love might have seemed conditional, making you feel like you need to put in extra effort to earn it. Remember, love is truly unconditional and deserves to be freely given and received.

Mars in the **Sixth House** reflects a strong desire to work diligently, but remember to rest and avoid pushing yourself too hard. Your motivation is closely linked to your daily activities and work efforts, which can be quite fulfilling. It's good to be mindful of managing your reactions, especially anger, to prevent it from turning inward, which might lead to feelings of depression or frustration.

You thrive on completing tasks and naturally feel energized when you're making progress. Sometimes, you might push yourself beyond your limits, so it's important to listen to your body to prevent burnout or irritability. The feeling of being busy and checking things off your list makes you feel alive! You probably enjoy taking on leadership roles, especially in lively, fast-paced, or physically active environments. Staying active, working out, and taking care of your body can be wonderful parts of your daily routine.

Routines might feel a bit challenging unless there's a meaningful reason to stick with them. Sitting still for long periods can be tough because you thrive on movement and productivity. This placement often instills a proactive, determined attitude at work, making you feel competitive and eager to take on your responsibilities. If you have pets, they might be lively, energetic, or sometimes a bit spirited, and likely feisty.

Jupiter in the **Sixth House** shows that you're energetic and often bring positivity and kindness into your daily routines, your health, and your efforts to help others. You tend to push yourself to the limit in everyday life, which might sometimes cause stress. You're always busy, with something on your plate. Finding moments of balance could really help you feel more centered.

You prosper when your activities feel purposeful or when you're making a difference, often going the extra mile to support others:

sometimes even taking on too much. This placement often makes you the go-to person for advice and encouragement, naturally lifting up those around you. Your physical health is usually good, but if there are challenging aspects in your chart, health issues might come up. You tend to overcommit or say yes too often, so learning to set healthy boundaries can be especially important for your well-being and growth.

Many good things can come your way through your daily efforts, opening doors for growth or new opportunities in your work or personal life. You probably love learning new skills or expanding your knowledge, especially if it helps you serve others better. Pets are likely a big source of joy for you and can even bring a sense of spiritual connection into your life. You may have several animals or multiple of the same type, like a few cats or dogs.

With **Saturn** in the **Sixth House**, you really value your daily responsibilities and approach them with a serious attitude. It's common to sometimes feel overwhelmed by work or health-related tasks, but this shows your strong sense of dedication. You tend to carry a lot and can feel the weight of your obligations, whether in your career, health, or everyday life. There's often a belief that true success comes from hard work and sacrifice, which makes you incredibly dependable, though occasionally prone to overdoing it or being too hard on yourself.

You are focused and methodical when your days are organized with clear goals, and others often look to you for support. Just remember to watch out for perfectionism and stress, as these issues can sometimes lead to physical strain. You might find fulfillment in roles that involve managing systems, caring for others, or working quietly behind the scenes with great commitment. When it comes to pets, Saturn here suggests you see animals as serious, lifelong friends. You might have fewer pets, but the ones you do have are cherished with deep loyalty and often become lasting companions.

Uranus in the **Sixth House** shows that your daily life is anything but predictable. You thrive on versatility! While you cherish your independence, you also find joy in community and helping others, or sometimes receiving support yourself. Rigid plans might not suit you best, so a bit of flexibility and variety in your routines can make your days more enjoyable. Doing the same thing every day can feel overwhelming or even cause anxiety, so it's a relief when your schedule allows for spontaneous moments or new ideas. You might be drawn to unconventional jobs, remote work, or non-traditional hours that give you the freedom you crave.

Having freedom in your workspace and daily activities is crucial to you, and you might find that you hop between jobs because you don't enjoy confining yourself to standard norms. Your thoughts might sometimes be unconventional or even a bit irrational, which adds to your unique perspective. Your approach to health and wellness could be quite distinctive too, possibly favoring holistic or alternative methods that others might find unusual compared to mainstream medicine. Sometimes, you might experience sudden health changes or unexpected work shifts, and learning how to go with the flow can be an essential part of your personal growth. When it comes to pets, you're likely to be drawn to animals that are rare, quirky, or in need of rescue, and if you decide to have a pet, you enjoy embracing their uniqueness with love.

Having **Neptune** in the **Sixth House** connects your daily life, work, and health with your imagination, creativity, intuition, and sometimes confusion. Your everyday experiences feel dreamy and inspiring, filled with beauty. At the same time, there might be a tendency to seek escapism in your routines, as you sometimes feel the need to retreat from reality. Your caring nature is drawn to helping others through creative or healing avenues like art, music, spiritual practices, design, or caregiving.

Since you're really attuned to the energy around you, creating a workspace that feels peaceful and inspiring is so helpful. Chaotic settings or strict routines might leave you feeling a bit drained or lost, so finding a balance can make a big difference. You might also find it challenging to set boundaries at work, sometimes taking on too much or sacrificing your own well-being to help others. Prioritizing self-care is key! In terms of health, you might experience issues doctors find hard to pinpoint and are often related more to emotional or spiritual stress rather than physical symptoms that a doctor can see. When it comes to pets, you form strong, deep emotional and even psychic bonds with animals. They tend to be like emotional healers in your life, and you could be naturally drawn to rescue work or caring for pets that need a little extra love and kindness.

Pluto in the **Sixth House** brings a top-secret and intense energy to your daily life, work, and health. You prefer to keep your routines private, viewing them as personal time. If you choose to move quietly or enjoy doing things solo, that's perfectly natural for you. Major changes in your work or health over time can inspire you to reinvent yourself or discover your inner strength through what others might see as simple routines. You carry a commanding presence at work and may be naturally drawn to roles like research, crisis response, psychology, or healing.

This placement can give you a sharp focus and a desire to control your routines, but it's important to watch out for power struggles or obsessive tendencies. You might get fully absorbed in perfecting your daily routine or withdraw completely; finding a healthy balance is essential. With pets, you tend to form deep, loyal bonds that help you heal emotional wounds and teach you about trust and resilience. Your relationship with pets having Pluto here is rarely casual; they are your soul companions.

7th House: The House of Partnerships & One-on-One Relationships

Ruler: Libra
Third Quadrant (Houses 7–9): Social & External Relationships

The 7th house is all about your close partnerships, such as your marriage, business collaborations, that one-on-one connection, and even your open enemies. It can give you clues about where and how you'll meet your future spouse, and what your long-term relationships might look like. This house also reflects how you see yourself through your interactions with others and your pursuit of balance and harmony. It shows what you want in committed relationships and how you connect with people. As it's ruled by Libra and overseen by Venus, this house kicks off the Third Quadrant, which focuses on your relationships and your role in society. Essentially, it represents your close partnerships, marriage, and business alliances.

While the First Quadrant explores personal identity and the Second Quadrant focuses on your inner world, the Third Quadrant shifts attention outward. It invites you to discover how you connect with others and navigate social agreements. This house offers valuable lessons in finding balance, maintaining peace, and embracing the art of compromise, revealing parallels that help you see yourself more clearly. Here, you learn about the importance of give-and-take, mutual respect, and meaningful interactions, all supporting your social growth and personal development through collaboration.

The 7th house is where you meet others. It's about long-term partnerships. Whether it's romantic relationships, business collaborations, or partnerships, it's all about connection. This house also relates to legal agreements and reflects how you approach intimate relationships, highlighting the qualities you seek or naturally attract in others. It can even symbolize "open enemies" or those who challenge you, helping you gain a clearer understanding of yourself. Think of this house as balancing the self-focused 1st house by gently asking: How do you relate to, compromise with, and work with others?

If **Sagittarius** is your **Rising** Sign, Gemini likely guides your 7th House. You're naturally drawn to witty, intelligent partners who keep your mind lively and engaged. You enjoy feeling like you're sharing knowledge with your partner, and that they're teaching you just as much. Shared experiences hold special importance for you, and you're not picky about physical types; instead, you're attracted to someone who can challenge your thoughts and keep conversations vibrant. Good communication means everything, and you don't do well with people who aren't engaging or stimulating, might not hold your interest long.

You might love a bit of variety and lively chats in your relationships. This placement can often bring several romances, sometimes short-term flings. It's easy to fall for someone quickly, but just as fast, you might get the ick and want to step away. When someone tries to commit, it might throw you off at first. However, you might find yourself more ready for commitment later in life after exploring what truly excites your mind and heart.

It's possible to have multiple marriages or partnerships throughout your life with this placement. The Gemini 7th House tends to attract musicians, writers, readers, intellectuals, tech lovers, gamers, speakers, multitaskers, and storytellers. You probably have many close one-on-one relationships. In your professional life, you're great at partnerships with family, friends, colleagues, and other individuals. You likely know people from all over, and traveling often helps keep you connected to loved ones. At times, you might feel lonely even when you're around others, which can make you feel vulnerable or distant. Learning how to navigate relationships is often a lifelong journey, but having someone willing to grow with you can make the path much easier.

Having the **Sun** in your **Seventh House** means your sense of self is deeply associated with your personal relationships. You often feel most vibrant and purposeful when you're married or in a committed relationship. You love the company of others and are truly seeking a long-term partner. This placement gives you qualities similar to Libra, known for their diplomacy and charm. You value fairness and harmony in your connections.

You're organically attracted to confident, charismatic people who inspire you or reflect qualities you admire. Your partners often reflect your strengths and vulnerabilities, helping you learn more about yourself. There's a heartfelt desire to be seen, chosen, and appreciated by your loved ones, which might sometimes lead you to give too much of yourself or depend heavily on their validation. Still, this placement reminds us that true balance begins with loving and understanding ourselves. When you honor your own needs alongside your partner's, your relationships can become even more fulfilling.

Additionally, the skills you develop through these partnerships can help you excel as a business partner. You're the kind of person who enjoys collaborating with others or managing a joint venture. You're great at forming genuine one-on-one connections by bringing peace and harmony to those around you.

In astrology, the Sun also represents the father or a father figure. In your seventh house, your relationship with your father or a father figure might have been especially creative, possibly even turning into a close friendship. From him, you may have learned a lot about love and business relationships, if this influence is well-aspected and aligns with your house sign.

Having the **Moon** in your **Seventh House**, your emotional happiness and connections revolve around close relationships. The Moon seeks safety, harmony, comfort, and emotional grounding through the exchange of intimate bonds with others. You feel most fulfilled when your relationships are built on mutual care and understanding. You tend to pick up on your partner's feelings and needs, often putting harmony above all else. Your nurturing instinct draws in those who are looking for emotional depth.

However, it's important to be mindful of setting boundaries, as over-relying on others can sometimes lead to codependency or people-pleasing. If relationships become unstable, it can cause you feelings of anxiety or depression, making self-regulation a top-tier priority. You crave relationships that offer consistency and emotional safety, where you feel validated. You're drawn to expressive, open-hearted individuals or those in need of nurturing. At times, you might also attract partners who seem emotionally distant, which offers opportunities for personal reflection. There can be a subconscious attraction to partners who mirror your early childhood dynamics, whether they are comforting or chaotic.

These relationship undercurrents can stir up old emotional wounds but also offer powerful opportunities for healing. You're supportive and excel in roles such as counseling or working in client relations, where your emotional intelligence shines. Your ability to understand others deeply and provide comfort is a real gift. Ultimately, your relationships are for your personal growth, helping you learn to love yourself just as much as you love others. In astrology, the Moon often represents the mother; for you, she might have been like a caring friend and supporter. Alternatively, if that wasn't your story because of harsh aspects, perhaps you sometimes felt rejected and sought validation elsewhere. Either way, she was probably creative, friendly, and valued balance in her relationships and life.

Mercury in your **7th House** means your relationships thrive on communication, connection, and mental stimulation. Your thoughts often reflect the energy of others, and you think best through dialogue and interaction when you are engaging with someone else. Your relationships often influence your communication style. You're the type of person who needs to talk about what's on your mind and get your thoughts out into the universe; love, conflict, plans, or ideas, whatever it is you just want to express yourself, and you seek a partner who can meet you at the same level of conversation. Speaking your truth will attract the right relationships and opportunities.

You're probably drawn to people who are sharp, clever, and mentally quick or opinionated. You like smart individuals who can relate to you. Relationships may move quickly, often starting with a strong intellectual connection or through written or spoken communication. You love to talk and converse, so you likely feel most connected during steady exchanges. You can see both sides of a situation and understand the balance from different perspectives.

You're a natural problem solver in your partnerships and may be someone who does great when working closely with someone, whether through writing, speaking, or business. However, you sometimes overthink or overanalyze your connections too much. Learning to listen fully, not just with your mind but with your heart, is crucial for building lasting intimacy.

Having **Venus** in your **Seventh House** really explains how love plays a heartfelt role in your life's journey! I mean it! You are seeking a love that lasts the long haul. You value trust and loyalty in your relationships. It might not always be an easy placement if you're after something serious, especially if others are just looking for something casual. But overall, your life is filled with love and beauty.

You have a charming, down-to-earth personality that makes it easy for you to build committed relationships. Deep emotional bonds matter a lot to you, and you're drawn to meaningful one-on-one partnerships. As a hopeless romantic, you dream of relationships that are both beautiful and balanced. You often attract attractive, stylish, or artistic people, and you might value appearance and chemistry in your connections. You're willing to compromise and keep the peace, but sometimes that means avoiding difficult conversations or hiding your true feelings.

You want love to feel like a fairy tale, but real intimacy means being vulnerable, even when it gets messy. You're naturally inclined toward partnership and do well working closely with someone, especially in close settings like business. Remember, the love you're seeking can also be found within yourself. While many with this placement find it easy to attract love and build partnerships, others may struggle to enjoy being single because they often tie their self-worth to being in a relationship. Venus in the 7th House craves that strong connection, harmony, and a mutual affection, but the key lesson here is to feel whole on your own so that love becomes a choice, not a necessity. Make sure to love yourself first.

Having **Mars** in your **Seventh House** means your relationships are full of passion and high intensity. These partnerships often begin spontaneously, which can sometimes test your emotional stability. You tend to prefer love that is either all in or all out; there's rarely a middle ground. You're drawn to bold and impulsive individuals who match your energetic spirit.

In relationships, you might find yourself with assertive or even competitive partners who motivate you and help you grow. You may initially feel friction or tension as you and your partner learn to work with this energy and take responsibility for both of your actions. With patience and effort, you can come together to build a strong and meaningful connection rather than conflict. Passionate arguments or heated debates can sometimes be a unique way of bonding, but it's important to remember that fighting isn't the same as closeness. You might seem calmer or diplomatic in public, but in one-on-one relationships, your true intensity shines through. This could be because you struggle with asserting yourself, which sometimes provokes angry reactions. Learning how to be assertive without anger is key. You really are your best self when you and your partner work toward shared goals or actively build something together. Physical intimacy and shared activities are essential.

Having **Jupiter** in your **Seventh House** suggests that your relationships are full of growth and important lessons. You have a strong faith in love, which tends to draw people in who help broaden your view of the world. Some with Jupiter in the 7th house enjoy very active love lives, while others prefer solitude, are lifelong bachelors or bachelorettes, sometimes choosing travel and independence over romance. You might be drawn to partners from diverse cultures, ethnicities, religions, spiritual paths, or life philosophies, which adds excitement and richness to your personal connections.

This can sometimes lead to power struggles because Jupiter values independence and hates being boxed in or forced to change. It's imperative to come together to share and experience without sacrificing personal values. You often attract partners with larger-than-life personalities or successful people who want to show you the world through shared experiences. Getting married quickly or eloping on a whim is quite common with this placement.

There's also the possibility of experiencing multiple marriages, as Jupiter is associated with amplification and abundance. Your approach to relationships is very generous, and you tend to put your heart into everything and see the best in people. Sometimes, this means you might give a little too much or see potential in others that isn't quite there yet. It's possible you could have more than one meaningful partnership over your lifetime, each one teaching you valuable lessons and helping you get closer to your true self. Usually, long-term commitment comes later, built on shared values and a sense of purpose. The most important thing is to stay grounded and avoid idealizing your relationships to the point of missing any red flags along the way.

Saturn in your **Seventh House** suggests that your relationships might feel like they come with a weight or a wait. What I mean here is you may be a late bloomer in the love department. Love may not always come easily, and you might experience delays, karmic lessons, rewards, or heavy responsibilities connected to your partnerships. You may attract older, more mature, or emotionally reserved partners. You might often take on the role of the "stable one" in your relationships.

At the beginning of your dating journey, it's common to feel that relationships might not meet your expectations or leave you feeling a bit unfulfilled. Sometimes, you might find yourself dating people who aren't very kind or with whom you don't share many interests. External factors can also make dating more challenging, and it's natural to feel disconnected at times. Just remember to pay attention to those red flags.

All of these experiences teach you to set clear boundaries and standards. Once you recognize your worth, stay patient, and remain open to vulnerability, you can eventually build something lasting. You don't take relationships lightly, but when you commit, it's often for life. The challenge is learning to balance structure with softness; love doesn't have to be a heavy burden or a chore. Release the idea that you must be perfect to be loved because nobody is. Your most meaningful relationships will be with those who accept both your human flaws and your commitment.

Having **Uranus** in your **Seventh House** suggests that love doesn't follow traditional rules. You desire freedom and excitement in your relationships and partnerships, where both of you maintain your individuality. You might attract partners who are unpredictable, rebellious, eccentric, unreliable, or unconventional. You resist being confined by traditional roles, and your relationships often mirror that attitude.

This can show up as long-distance relationships, non-traditional arrangements, or sudden starts and stops in love. You and your partner may have many unpredictable experiences together. There's a restless energy here that makes commitment difficult until you find someone who truly understands your need for space and self-expression. You can also be the partner who sparks change by showing others how to love without feeling controlled. The challenge is balancing your need for independence with your desire for deep connection. Once you find someone who supports your growth and isn't threatened by your individuality, you can build a relationship that feels genuinely authentic.

If **Neptune** is in your **Seventh House**, you're a dreamer and very imaginative when it comes to love. You're a passionate dreamer who often becomes very creative in your relationships. You tend to idealize your partner or the idea of a perfect relationship, longing for a soulful and meaningful bond. Peace, love, and acceptance are important to you in partnerships.

Neptune here adds a bit of fogginess to how you see and experience relationships, often attracting artistic, creative, or emotionally complex people who inspire your imagination. Sometimes, you might fall for someone's potential rather than seeing them clearly, wearing rose-colored glasses. It's helpful to be cautious about keeping people around who don't truly have your best interests at heart, and to avoid putting others on a pedestal. Boundaries might feel a little hazy, and you could find yourself giving too much or losing sight of yourself in love, especially if reality doesn't match your romantic values. Still, there's a remarkable ability for spiritual love and an unfathomable emotional connection when you stay grounded.

Your relationships can be filled with synchronicity, creativity, or healing energy. You and your partner may share similar backgrounds or coping styles, sometimes experiencing shared challenges or traumas. There might also be tendencies toward codependency, but the lesson is to learn how to love deeply without losing yourself. When your love life is balanced, this placement can lead to a soulful connection that feels perfectly timed.

Having **Pluto** in your **Seventh House** indicates that your approach to love is intense, not superficial. You could encounter powerful relationships that may challenge you to your core. These relationships reflect you, revealing parts of yourself you might otherwise avoid, and offer vital lessons through close, one-on-one connections. You might attract enigmatic or powerful partners, or those who push you to explore your emotional depths.

Such relationships feel destined or emotionally overwhelming. A fear of betrayal is common, mainly when it stems from those closest to you. This placement also suggests that your partners may become obsessive, even after a breakup, rooted in jealousy and control issues. However, these experiences teach you to assert your power without dominance.

8th House: The House of Transformation & Shared Resources

Ruler: Scorpio
Third Quadrant (Houses 7–9): Social & External Relationships

The 8th House is where things get really, really deep in your chart. This is where life changes happen. This house rules over sharing, intimacy, sex, the occult, mental health, shared finances, emotional merging, inheritance, debts, energetic exchange, and the concept of death and rebirth, not always literal, but symbolic through cycles of endings and transformations that shape us and define who we become in life. This is the house of what we receive through death. It reveals how you handle vulnerability, power, truth, control, and letting go.

The 8th House is also where you confront parts of life that are taboo or uncomfortable for you, which will be revealed. Any secrets or hidden things are brought into the light here. It's the shadow work house placement. It guides our emotional survival skills, such as how we process grief and loss when we experience it, all the way to how we navigate the union of mine and yours and turning it into "ours." This house can also show how you receive support from others, whether it's financially or sexually, and how you deal with trust, betrayal, and any karmic ties you might have. This is the house of self-development.

If **Scorpio** is your **Rising** sign, Gemini likely influences your Eighth House. This means your revitalization often comes through communication and your understanding of things. You might find that your emotional experiences are best processed by talking with friends, writing your thoughts down, or mentally exploring your feelings. You could be exceptionally talented at shadow work, bravely facing uncomfortable truths and things from your past, and transforming into a better version of yourself. Just remember, there's a chance you might feel overwhelmed or even experience some lows if your dedication to this work and mastering your skills becomes too intense. Make sure to take breaks. Embrace your journey with kindness toward yourself and give yourself grace.

If you're not careful, it's easy to overlook other important parts of life. Sometimes, this can lead to feelings of anxiety and mental blocks. Remember, healing is possible through ways like therapy, journaling, or learning, especially when you're uncovering secrets or exploring taboo topics most dare not touch. You're naturally curious and have a desire to understand everything. From sex and intimacy to the mysteries of life and death, you are wanting to fully grasp it all.

You might sometimes find yourself analyzing your feelings too much, scratching the surface rather than exploring their full emotional depth. It's normal to ask those crucial questions, but then avoid the most difficult answers. Don't hesitate to ask, though, because your words hold power and truth. Doing this helps you inspire others, too. You have a wonderful gift for words, whether in conversations, teaching, or storytelling, assisting others to understand their inner shadows or deep dark secrets. You may experience several "deaths" in your life. You might have some rocky identity shifts, heartbreaking breakups, or stressful career changes. Each time, you emerge wiser and more in tune with your true self.

If your **Sun** is in the **Eighth House**, you might find yourself sharing some Scorpio traits. Your sense of identity is strongly linked with change and mystery, making life intriguing. Your youngest memories may include moments of loss or death, whether from childhood or a personal experience; either way, these events likely took place early in your life. You might also prefer not to display your emotions openly, perhaps because you experience them so deeply already.

You tend to express your feelings when you're alone, unless you're with someone you trust completely. You're not content with just skimming the surface of things; you're here to grow and deepen your understanding, which means facing challenges that many people tend to avoid. You're naturally drawn to life's mysteries, whether it's through building close relationships, exploring topics like death, delving into the mind or spirituality, confronting trauma, or studying psychology. I mention intimacy first because it involves sharing energy or finances with another person, emphasizing the importance of connection.

Throughout your life, you might experience several phases of personal growth and change. As you continue to evolve, others may not always see the same version of you, and that's perfectly okay. Everyone has their own unique journey. You crave a meaningful connection that goes beyond just the physical; you long for a bond that truly touches your soul. When someone genuinely sees and understands you, it can feel like your entire heart is open and at ease, creating a beautiful, heartfelt bond.

While that can feel frightening, it also reveals where your true strength lies, through vulnerability. You might be drawn to occult or spiritual sciences such as astrology, tarot, numerology, or palmistry, and you may have spiritual gifts, perhaps even a psychic ability. You're probably good at keeping secrets, both for yourself and for others. You may notice tendencies toward addiction or a higher sex drive, as well. This placement also suggests a very strong intuition. Your finances and romantic relationships may fluctuate, especially with the Sun in the 8th House; you might inherit money from a loved one's passing. In astrology, the Sun often represents the father or a paternal figure. Your father might have been very controlling, intense, and protective, which could have led to commanding behavior. For some, he might not have been present, or he might have passed away.

Having the **Moon** in your **Eighth House** means your emotional world is incredibly rich and hidden. It can feel like a rollercoaster because you experience your feelings very intensely, especially around trust, vulnerability, and loss. These strong emotions make everything feel meaningful. The Moon here also emphasizes uncovering secrets and illuminating hidden things. Sometimes this placement might seem a bit distant or cold, but it's all part of your journey to better understand yourself.

You might have gone through emotional trauma or loss early on, which has influenced how you connect with others. It's natural to crave closeness, even while fearing potential hurt or betrayal. Deep down, you desire someone who sees and accepts you fully, the good and the challenging parts, including your darker side. This placement can suggest strong fertility, though it might come with some complications.

It also grants you strong intuitive abilities or even psychic abilities. You might experience psychic dreams that feel so real, they seem prophetic. You could find yourself curious about the supernatural and the occult, or perhaps your mother is as well. Maybe you both share a more holistic perspective on life. You're attuned to picking up on others' energies even before they say a word, making you quite perceptive.

Your emotional sensitivity can make you feel guarded or like shutting down when things seem unsafe. It's invaluable to learn to manage your emotional waves so they don't overwhelm you. You might find it more comfortable to keep your feelings private and handle your emotions on your own, especially if you feel your emotions are too deep to share. Be mindful that a tendency toward addictive behaviors can arise from having obsessive thoughts, and you might try to drown things out as a way to cope. Remember, you're not alone, and with gentle support, you can find healthier ways to navigate these feelings.

In fortunate cases, the Moon can point to inheritances or family wealth. Engaging with your home environment by sharing financially can bring a warm sense of fulfillment. In astrology, the Moon represents the mother, and for you, she may have experienced some intense changes during your upbringing. Depending on the circumstances, you might have felt your needs weren't fully met in childhood, and maybe all you needed was a simple, comforting hug.

It's possible you've faced some emotional challenges, such as difficulties maintaining emotional stability or feeling connected with your mother. Perhaps you experienced losing your mother at a young age, or she might have been dealing with health issues or physical hardships during your childhood. Sometimes, having a mother who isn't mentally well or is very emotionally expressive can also impact your feelings and relationships.

Mercury in the **Eighth House** suggests your mind is eager to explore what's not seen and constantly processes that information. You're the investigator, the psychologist, the lover of taboo topics who seeks deeper understanding in every conversation. You want to discuss death, the occult, astrology, and maintain a profound dialogue. Small talk isn't your thing; you want to learn about your partner's trauma history, their greatest fears, and what keeps them awake at night.

Do you ever talk to the other side? You might find it easy to do so and see what's concealed behind closed doors. You're adept at sensing when someone is hiding something, which can drive you crazy. You may even have a gift for reading people or picking up on unspoken clues. You can read between the lines or even pick up on others' thoughts.

You're mentally sharp and naturally intuitive. This placement often points to someone who contemplates life's big themes: death, intimacy, trust, betrayal. You might enjoy researching mysterious topics, therapy, or criminal psychology. You could even turn this interest into a career focused on exploring the human psyche.

When it comes to communication, you're very selective about who you share your energy with. This selectiveness is protective rather than mean; some might perceive your communication style as sterile or cold. You prefer to listen first to gauge if it's safe to share your ideas. If you have this placement, you might also struggle with issues like depression or mental illness. This can cause mental chaos and feel exhausting at times. You may not realize when you become mentally drained, often because you're overwhelmed.

Venus in the **Eighth House** means that love is all or nothing for you. You don't do it halfway. You desire a love that consumes you and transforms you. A love that feels like two souls fused together as one. One-night stands and casual flings might seem empty because what you truly crave is deep intimacy and loyalty from another person.

People are drawn to your aura and energy, making you a magnetic, seductive force field without even realizing it. Not in all cases, but some might attract intense, powerful lovers, who could also be dishonest or unfaithful partners who stir emotional chaos in your life. In some cases, this could even result in you becoming a widow. You might marry someone who was widowed or divorced, as well.

Your experience with love may unfold in different ways. You're the type who can fall deeply in love but can also get caught up in power struggles, jealousy, obsession, or controlling your partner. In the best scenarios, there's an opportunity to learn how to trust and love fully or to be completely immersed with your partner in healthy, positive ways.

Some people with this placement might use their charm and beauty to gain money or resources from others, since the 8th house governs other people's money, unlike the 2nd house, which governs your own. Others may feel compelled to give you gifts, or you might combine finances with a partner. It's possible to benefit financially from relationships, marry someone with significant wealth, or work in finance. There may even be financial debts owed to you in this lifetime.

If your **Mars** is in the **Eighth House**, your desires are secret and hidden. You have strong sexual energy, whether you carry it or have experienced being sexualized; either way, you possess an intensity and mystery that others notice immediately and can sense. You may overindulge in physical and sensual pleasures. You hide who you truly are from others, or most of what makes you, you.

This is only because you put up a wall of defense, blocking out anyone who might not understand you and giving yourself a sense of protection. You fear betrayal and know that pain would cut deeply into your soul if it were ever felt. There's a drive for familiarity and a strong desire for control, which can lead to power struggles in your partnerships or dating life. There is a give-and-take kind of energy here.

In relationships, you bring passion and drive, but you might sometimes struggle with feelings like jealousy or obsession. You might feel quite possessive of your loved ones, especially when you're emotionally vulnerable. It's understandable to sometimes feel psychologically self-destructive with these feelings to some degree. You have a resilient survival instinct, and life may throw curveballs your way that test your strength, especially in matters of love and finances. Remember, your strength helps you direct these moments.

You may attract lovers who are dominant or even a little dangerous, but what you're truly seeking is someone who can match your depth and intensity. It's important to find healthy ways to manage your energy and channel it into something positive. Engaging in activities that allow you to defend yourself, stay active, or use your body in a controlled environment would be beneficial. You have a desire for passion and loyalty. Once you learn how to assert yourself without overpowering others and how to lower your guard without losing your strength, your relationships can become healing.

If your **Jupiter** is in the **Eighth House**, it means you may receive support through financial matters such as an inheritance, a trust, gifts, or sometimes even your partner's resources. You might get money that you didn't necessarily have to work for by having Jupiter here in the 8th. Throughout your life, you will form many strong connections, learn how to heal yourself, and grow through transformation and shared intimacy with others. You may even receive some unexpected gifts along the way.

Speaking of "gifts," you can be drawn to subjects that most consider taboo, like sex, spirituality, astrology, mysticism, occult sciences, psychology, and death. These may become significant influences in your life. This is a very spiritual placement, and it's not uncommon to have many gifts that connect you to the other side. You could be a natural medium or guru.

You have a natural potential to be a wonderful spiritual teacher or counselor, serving as a healer in your place. With Jupiter associated with luck and the 8th house often linked to death, your experiences might manifest in various ways. Sometimes, luck comes after a loss, or you might go through many endings in life, many deaths, from actual deaths to the conclusion of relationships. You could also go through many personal renewals yourself. This placement often encourages you to reflect on what life is.

Give yourself patience to discover what you truly believe. You have a lot to offer in relationships, but be cautious not to overgive, rescue, or try to fix others. Your generosity is beautiful, but it needs boundaries. Be mindful of tendencies toward addiction, as some may want to drown out their gifts, dreams, or life experiences a little too much.

Saturn in the **Eighth House** means you don't take intimacy lightly. There's a cautious, serious, heavy energy here around trust, intimacy, shared finances, or emotional openness. You may feel confined or afraid to truly let someone in. This can stem from early experiences of betrayal, loss, abandonment, or emotional repression.

You might have learned early on that you need to protect yourself, so it can take time (or pain) to open up to others genuinely. In extreme cases, this placement can also reflect the loss of a father during early childhood, having a neglectful or absent father, or an emotionally repressive father, possibly even struggling with substance abuse. You may have to overcome mental health issues because you need to master discipline, self-control, and responsibility, which could ultimately bring you financial rewards through marriage or legal matters.

There may be karmic lessons related to authority, intimacy, control, and support. You won't get away with the same things others do, and you might learn the hard way first, but you do eventually learn. You may attract partners who challenge you to build stronger emotional boundaries or confront your fears of closeness. You might have experienced financial instability growing up, but as you focus on your passions, you will be rewarded for your efforts in the end.

Have patience and trust that it will come. You may harbor an early inner fear of loss and a resistance to change. But once you do the work, Saturn rewards you with the purest, most enduring form of intimacy. Over time, you learn how to manage shared resources, understand emotional responsibility, and embrace your emotional depth with structure and refinement.

Uranus in the **Eighth House** can really shake things up in life by bringing the themes of the 8th house more suddenly and unexpectedly. You might experience sudden endings and new beginnings, especially related to financial support or emotional attachments. Think of unexpected changes and bizarre accidents. You may have been in a strange situation that caught you completely off guard and turned your world completely upside down.

Uranus adds unpredictability and, depending on its influence, helps you defy the odds. Unexpected financial shifts are familiar with this placement. Your path is anything but predictable. You're here to break the rules around sex, money, authority, and emotional vulnerability.

Receiving unexpected money could happen through this placement, perhaps from an inheritance you weren't aware of. You might sometimes feel a bit like an outsider, unsure of where you truly belong. Your love life could be quite unique and open, involving long-distance connections, exciting bedroom experiments, or multiple partners. You might also hesitate to dive into deep intimacy because you're afraid of losing your independence. Additionally, you may find yourself questioning your beliefs or even rebelling against them, exploring a different path when it comes to spirituality if that's something you're interested in.

You're the black sheep because you're not like everyone else, and that makes you special. You're also a catalyst for positive change. You help others break free from toxic patterns, and in doing so, life guides your own journey for growth. Remember, true intimacy is built on trust, not control. When you meet someone who accepts your wild, quirky side and encourages your development, you can create a relationship that allows you to experience real depth and warmth.

When **Neptune** is placed in the **Eighth House**, it often brings a mystical and sometimes dreamy feel to your relationships and personal growth. You might experience a deep spiritual connection with your partner, dreaming of merging your souls as one. It's common to romanticize your partners or the idea of a union, and boundaries may sometimes feel a bit tricky. You could find yourself giving a lot in relationships or absorbing your partner's emotional struggles as if they were your own.

You are very intuitive. Maybe to the point that you might struggle to distinguish between what's real and otherworldly energy. You could also have psychic gifts, especially in sensing people's implicit feelings or energies. Expect intense or lucid dreams and learn to balance your visions with reality, keeping your heart open without losing yourself.

Exploring your spirituality is essential, and with this placement, you might become obsessed with topics related to the 8th house, such as life and death. You may idealize sex or put it on a pedestal and might have tendencies toward escapism, possibly involving substances. If this resonates with you, it's essential to set some boundaries. These are just a few ways this placement could influence your life.

Pluto in the **Eighth House** is on a whole new level when it comes to finances, transformation, spiritual gifts, and inheritances. This part of your chart represents where you make a significant change in your life. Where you kill off the old versions of yourself and emerge better than before, you may have experienced life in intense ways, including trauma related to acts of love, sex, death, and shared finances.

You've been through a lot. You might face themes of loss, abandonment, or issues of control in your life or past life. You are strong and possess the power to change through it all. You learn how to confront emotional power struggles directly, reclaim your power, and use it for healing.

You may attract (or become) someone who is commanding, secretive, or even obsessive. Your relationships are often karmic and passionate, but they can also trigger your deepest fears, leading to your most tremendous growth. You're the alchemist, psychologist, mystic, and the one who turns pain into wisdom and trauma into strength. You have an interest in the taboo, the occult, and the spiritual world. When you learn to release control and trust the process, you become an unstoppable force of healing, not just for yourself but for others as well.

9th House: The House of Higher Beliefs & Education

Ruler: Sagittarius
Third Quadrant (Houses 7–9): Social & External Relationships

The 9th house governs your higher education, philosophy, long-distance travel, spirituality, and your life's purpose. It's about exploring the world both physically and mentally through learning about different cultures, religions, and belief systems. This house expands your horizons and introduces you to new perspectives. It's a joyful house that carries a soul-based teacher energy.

This is the place where you're encouraged to explore the big questions: Why am I here? What is the point? The 9th House invites you to step outside your comfort zone, whether it's through travel, learning, or spiritual discovery. It's about what you believe in, how you see freedom and adventure, and your openness to taking risks on your path of personal growth. This is where your connection with the divine begins. It's also where journeys, whether physical or metaphorical, help you embrace new experiences that shape your identity and transform the way you see the world around you.

If **Sagittarius** is your **Rising** sign, Leo probably influences your Ninth House. Your outlook on the world is wonderfully shaped by your love of discovering new things. You're naturally curious and excited about exploring long-distance travel or trying out new skills. You have a thirst for knowledge that often leads you to learn new languages, explore different philosophies, or enjoy lively intellectual conversations.

You tend to do well in your studies and love astrology and philosophy. You're enthusiastic about understanding the world around you and feel the most confident when you inspire others. Your journey is about finding a personal philosophy that genuinely resonates with you and that feels right. You love to share what you learn with others. Reading books to expand your mind would do wonders for you.

Having the **Sun** in the **Ninth House** indicates a strong identification with your beliefs and a zest for exploration and growth. The Sun loves to be in here, and you shine the brightest when you're expanding your horizons. Whether you're learning something new, sharing your knowledge with others, or exploring different places, that's when you feel at your very best.

With the Sun in the 9th house, you have a joyful and adventurous spirit, much like Sagittarius. You're friendly and warm, and you love connecting with others easily. Your curiosity about different cultures, philosophies, and spiritual journeys inspires you. You're fortunate, and situations often turn out positively for you. Your sense of self is greatly connected to exploring and understanding the meaning of life, making your journey truly significant.

You are truly the forever student or teacher. A naturally born mentor others look to for help and guidance. You may feel restless if you're stuck in a routine or surrounded by limited viewpoints. Your confidence grows as you broaden your horizons, and you come alive when you travel and meet people from different backgrounds.

You love teaching and sharing your knowledge. You are fascinated by life and eager to explore every aspect of it. In astrology, the Sun can represent the father or a father figure. Yours might have been someone who served as a teacher or philosopher of sorts. A person who enjoyed traveling, perhaps internationally, and was very outgoing. He could have come from a different background or spoken a different language.

The **Moon** in the **Ninth House** shows that your emotional happiness thrives when you're free to explore new ideas and places. You're truly genuine and optimistic, and your belief in the universe or whatever it might be brings you comfort and peace. This free-spirited nature means that travel and learning often nourish your soul. Your feelings about your beliefs may shift over time, sometimes causing frustration as your worldview evolves.

Perhaps you've been raised in a nurturing environment that encouraged curiosity or in a family with strong beliefs. For you, emotional security often comes from understanding the bigger picture and feeling connected to something greater through exploring spirituality. That's where you find true fulfillment. You're quite emotionally intelligent and tend to want to do the right thing; following the law is essential to you, even if you occasionally rebel.

You're a romantic at heart, seeking truth in all aspects of life, sometimes even being called a guru. You may dream of traveling to places that hold special meaning for you or that make you feel whole, especially in diverse, multicultural environments. In astrology, the Moon also symbolizes the mother, and for you, she or women in your family might have brought you luck, wisdom, and abundance. Your mother may have been from a multicultural background or speak multiple languages, and she may be interested in traveling and continuing her learning. Growing up, you might have moved to another country, making home feel elusive as your soul yearns to explore everything.

When **Mercury** resides in the **Ninth House**, your focus centers on possibilities of life. You aim to uncover life's truth and meaning, and you enjoy exploring distant ideas. As a natural philosopher and communicator, you excel in grammar and learning, often craving more knowledge and showing interest in spirituality. You are intrigued by languages, cultures, and abstract concepts, and you think creatively and visionarily.

You're skilled at explaining complex topics, such as spirituality and intellectual subjects, and tend to discuss broad themes like faith, beliefs, and world issues. Be careful not to spread your mental energy too thin by trying to learn too many things simultaneously. Your innovative thinking can shape your beliefs into truth, and you can manifest ideas vocally by just speaking them aloud.

You may also have spiritual gifts, like receiving messages from guides, ancestors, or loved ones through intuition or dreams. Your words can inspire and motivate others, and you are often drawn to learning through communication. Some individuals with this placement become translators, teachers, philosophers, or study abroad students.

If you have **Venus** in the **Ninth House**, you're naturally lucky when it comes to spirituality and travel. You have a love for different cultures and enjoy embracing people from all kinds of backgrounds. I really love this about you, and as a Sagittarius Moon myself, I understand!

For you, soul connections are very meaningful, and you might find yourself on a heartfelt mission to meet a like-minded partner. You're often drawn to people whose lives are different from yours. This could be someone from another country, a person of a different religion, or someone from a culture outside your own upbringing. You might meet this special person right where you are, or through your travels.

Sometimes, your journeys take you to them, or they come into your life from afar. They might have different religious beliefs, which can challenge and inspire your own in even more exciting, positive ways. You also love learning, especially through your relationships, and you tend to connect deeply with partners who share your curiosity about knowledge. You want your lover to travel with you, try new things, embrace different beliefs with you, and take everything our planet has to offer, hand in hand. Love for you is truly an adventure and an incredible journey.

Having **Mars** in the **Ninth House** suggests that you follow your beliefs and passions with resilience. You are enthusiastic about traveling, learning, and gaining independence. You're adventurous and very courageous, though sometimes impulsive when exploring new places, philosophies, or ideas. Seriously, you are highly intelligent, and we all know it!

You are very sociable and dedicate a lot of energy to learning about various subjects. Your energy is best directed when you're traveling, taking on physical challenges, or engaging in intellectual debates. You could be the type to debate with your teachers growing up, often challenging their ideas. You might also be attracted to causes or philosophies that require you to stand up and fight for what you believe in.

Be mindful of a tendency to be strict or overly forceful when sharing your worldview, especially around people from different backgrounds who might not fully agree with you. You may be spiritually rebellious, having grown up one way and later entirely gone against the norm. You want to dive deep into learning about the world and different cultures. You might feel compelled to do missionary or charity work.

It's crucial for you to find your purpose in life so that life feels more meaningful to you and not just because you dislike wasting time, but because, without a belief system, everything can feel very empty. Having something to believe in is important, even if it's just yourself. Your mind is your greatest power; the more you learn, the more you feel aligned, aware, and are capable of transforming your reality.

If **Jupiter** is in your **Ninth House**, it's an excellent sign that luck is on your side, and you naturally embody the roles of an alchemist, guru, teacher, or writer. You might experience a significant life-changing moment that helps you discover your inner wisdom. You have so much luck and abundance around you. This placement really emphasizes your ability to attract good fortune by understanding that believing you already have it can help make it a reality. Essentially, you know and understand the natural law of attraction.

Since Jupiter rules over Sagittarius and the 9th house is also ruled by Sagittarius, this placement feels very much at home, but even more powerful. You have a special talent for expanding other people's minds in ways that make them really think about the world, even when you're simply just out with friends. When people talk about you, you effortlessly turn conversations into opportunities to teach without even trying; your words and vibe just flow naturally. You're likely to attract more chances for growth through education, travel, or spiritual journeys.

Your outlook on the world is open-minded, and you tend to stay optimistic about what life has to offer. Your generosity and faith can really inspire those around you. People see you as joyful, kind, and wise beyond your years. You might even love traveling to learn or teach, or just for fun, because your passion drives you. Plus, with this placement, you have a talent for fortune-telling and spiritual practices. Just remember to keep a balance so that your roomy energy doesn't overwhelm you.

If **Saturn** is in your **Ninth House**, it suggests you take your beliefs seriously and tend to have a disciplined, structured approach to learning. You might face academic challenges, such as setbacks, being held back, or encountering obstacles while attending college. This placement could also mean you hold multiple degrees, perhaps changing your mind or needing to persevere yourself to achieve the highest ones. Saturn often delays these outcomes, but patience and effort will eventually bring rewards, even if it takes longer.

Some individuals with this placement may dislike traditional schooling or prefer studying abroad. Many scenarios are possible, especially depending on aspects of this house. You might be an atheist or someone who questions conventional faith, needing to develop your own philosophy through personal experiences. You may also have a skeptical view of religion, perhaps because it was imposed upon you, and you could be interested in esoteric practices like astrology, palmistry, magic, or spiritual work.

This path could involve facing delays in higher education or travel, but ultimately lead to profound, practical wisdom. Learning patience and understanding the boundaries of your belief systems are essential. Be cautious of others trying to influence or manipulate you through philosophy or spirituality, especially those with conflicting values. If you're into traveling, the world can be a journey leading to self-discovery.

Uranus in your **Ninth House** might indicate that your worldview is unusual, controversial, and that you're drawn to radical ideas or alternative spiritual paths. Uranus is the planet of change, often sudden. You may abruptly shift your beliefs, not sticking to one religion, or discover that you are more spiritual than religious later in life. Unexpected travel opportunities could arise that might dramatically alter your life's course.

You might feel restless and resist outdated beliefs or traditional schooling methods. You could excel at teaching, helping others see different perspectives. You may find a new way to teach that leaves a meaningful impact. You prefer to learn through unique experiences, self-discovery, and figuring things out on your own.

Your innovative, out-of-the-box thinking often inspires others to see things differently. You are very inquisitive and tend to ask many questions. You might want to teach unusual topics or explore unfamiliar cultures. Here, you may experience back-and-forth feelings about all 9th house themes, meaning you could crave learning from multiple perspectives and then randomly disappear to find yourself. If you have the freedom to travel, learn, and connect with your spirituality, you will find peace.

Having **Neptune** in the **Ninth House** focuses on your open-minded approach to beliefs and spirituality. You often dream about exploring distant lands and may find yourself lucky enough to make those journeys happen. As a dreamer and optimist, your outlook on life and spirituality is inspiring and adventurous. Your beliefs tend to be flexible rather than rigid, and you naturally get along with people from diverse backgrounds because you're curious about their cultures and philosophies.

You love learning from their differences and are spiritually motivated by mystical experiences or the arts. Visiting foreign places helps deepen your spiritual and emotional self-awareness. You enjoy contemplating your higher purpose and are gifted at learning new languages. Traveling near water often brings you peace, and you're drawn to meditation, mysticism, or other ethereal experiences. However, there can sometimes be confusion or even deception regarding your beliefs, or you might experience betrayal related to higher knowledge or someone in a learning role.

It's important to stay alert and distinguish between what is real and what might be an illusion. You believe in acceptance and love for everyone as they are, embodying the spirit of Miss Congeniality, and your dream is for world peace. It would be wonderful if everyone could get along and realize that we are all from different backgrounds, and that this is probably shown in different ways. It is presented through culture, religion, upbringing, different backgrounds, and maybe even being taught differently. You get the gist, I'm sure. You are the kind of person who loves to learn and is deeply connected to your inner divine self.

Pluto in the **Ninth House** suggests that you are attracted to more taboo knowledge and may experience intense inner transformations through your spiritual or philosophical pursuits. You might be an atheist or someone who develops their own personal philosophy or worldview. You could encounter adventures, travel, gain exposure to different cultures, learning, and experience spirituality, all of which could significantly alter your life. A far away journey might completely change your outlook, helping you so much with personal growth beyond what you could imagine. Pursuing a degree could bring unprecedented abundance.

However, with Pluto, we often face experiences that totally transform us. Maybe someone took your power, or you feel as though they did, maybe in a religious or spiritual setting. You might struggle to see the world through a positive lens and may distrust authority figures or teachers. This could be because those you trusted with specific knowledge, a secret, or "the world" in general, let you down or betrayed your trust.

Yet, this is the house where you access your power. You reclaim your strength by learning more about life and different cultures, broadening your mind, and taking life-changing trips. You're not afraid to confront the darker sides of beliefs and are likely to question the meaning of life itself. Your experiences with learning and travel can greatly shape your identity and your view of the world. You may even help others change by sharing your insights.

10th House: The House of Public Life & Career

Ruler: Capricorn
Fourth Quadrant (Houses 10–12): Public Image & Life Path

The 10th house, also called the Midheaven (MC), sits at the top of your chart. It represents your career, ambitions, reputation, success, social standing, legacy, and how others see you in your community or workplace. It's the place where you shape your legacy and choose how you want the world to view you. This house also touches on authority figures and those who are "in charge," including your relationship with your father or parental figures.

The 4th house is all about nurturing, emotional roots, and private parental experiences, as well as your connection to home and family. On the other hand, the 10th house represents your public responsibilities, reputation, and how you'll be remembered. No matter if you're a storyteller, artist, teacher, healer, lawyer, or in another profession, the 10th house plays an important role in shaping that part of your life.

This house is ruled by Capricorn and overseen by Saturn. It marks the start of the Fourth Quadrant, which focuses on your place in the world: career, reputation, and legacy. Unlike the earlier, more personal quadrants, the Fourth Quadrant highlights your outer life and achievements. The 10th house reveals your public image and how you seek to leave your mark. Lessons learned here demand discipline and accountability. This house bridges your personal foundations from earlier quadrants to the broader world, showing how inner and outer life shape public identity.

The sign on your 10th-house cusp plays a significant role in shaping how you handle your reputation and what you bring to your professional life. It emphasizes the qualities others see in you and can influence your career journey. Ultimately, the 10th house gently reminds you to consider how your actions and achievements can become your meaningful contribution to the world.

If **Virgo** is your **Rising** Sign, Gemini probably influences your Tenth House, connecting your career and public image to your gift for communication. You really shine in roles that involve speaking, writing, teaching, performing, social media, or networking. Success for you might come from juggling different roles or trying out various paths until you find what truly fits your passion. Your adaptability and wide-ranging interests can make it tricky to choose just one career, since you excel in many areas.

Jobs that stimulate your mind and keep you engaged, like psychology or detective work, are often a good fit. Your natural charm and strong communication skills often lead you into leadership roles. Gemini MCs are attracted to socially related careers and thrive on variety and mental stimulation. The more you share and connect with others, the more your talents are appreciated, and your name becomes linked to something meaningful.

If you have your **Sun** in the **Tenth House**, your career and public image are central to your identity. You embody Capricorn energy, since your Sun is in the House ruled by this career-focused sign. You thrive the most when working toward your goals and being recognized for your contributions. Leadership comes naturally to you, and you often seek out positions of authority or guidance.

You want to make an impact, are very ambitious to do so, and desire to be remembered for something meaningful while earning your peers' respect. You may face obstacles along the way, possibly from a young age, which might have required you to "help out" or take on an independent role in the home. You may have started working early. You might explore different career paths or learn how to overcome career obstacles. To others in the public eye, you might seem like a workaholic, but that's just because you enjoy working hard.

Be mindful of taking on too much and overdoing it. Your self-identity is deeply connected to your professional achievements, so supporting your values through shadow work is vital. Having the Sun in the 10th gives you the gift of creativity and many talents, and it's generally a sign of potential fame. Since the MC (Midheaven) is the highest point in the chart and the Sun is in it, this is where you stand out publicly.

This can be a blessing or a challenge, depending on how you handle attention. You could excel as an artist, painter, actor, singer, musician,

206

fashion designer, or politician, though the cusp sign should also be considered. Make sure to blend both energies.

In astrology, the Sun often represents the father or a father figure. He can be a great source of inspiration for you, and you might have learned a lot from him, getting some support with your career. This placement might have brought your father into the spotlight, or maybe he was a workaholic, too. Overall, others see you as confident, successful, and driven.

If you have your **Moon** in the **Tenth House**, your career needs to be emotionally fulfilling as well as financially rewarding. You might be known for your empathy, strong emotional intelligence, nurturing leadership, or your ability to connect with others on a human level rather than seeing them as less than. You could also be recognized publicly and find yourself in the spotlight. Being publicly recognized can boost your mood, but it can also make you sensitive to criticism, especially regarding what you are known for or your legacy.

How you are perceived in society matters greatly to you, and you are very sensitive about how others see you. You genuinely want to make an impact on the world and help others. You care about people's opinions because you want to be liked, admired, and seen. You might find yourself in roles where you care for others, offer guidance, or take on leadership positions: trust your intuition when making decisions.

You could excel in nurturing careers, such as working from home, becoming a cook, caring for infants in a hospital, babysitting, or owning a daycare. Professions that are mostly female-dominated, like therapy or counseling, would suit you and provide emotional fulfillment. You also have a gift for spiritual work or even connecting with the other side.

In astrology, the Moon symbolizes the mother, and for you, she may have influenced your career choices or instilled a sense of responsibility that shaped who you are today. She might have motivated you to pursue your goals, guided you on how to achieve them, or been in the spotlight, just as the Sun in the 10th indicates that your father could have been. She could have been a workaholic or taken on the central provider role. It's also possible that your father was absent, either financially or in a broader sense, physically. You might find that your private or home life is exposed to the public.

If **Mercury** is in the **Tenth House**, your voice, ideas, and way of thinking play a special role in your career success and how you're remembered. You're naturally goal-minded and motivated by achieving long-term success and maintaining a good reputation. People often see you as someone who communicates a lot or speaks fast, but also as someone with a lot of knowledge. Even if you speak often, you truly know what you're talking about.

You have a voice that sounds like a leader and innovator. You succeed in careers involving speaking, public speaking, writing, education, broadcasting, communication, or exploration, whatever offers variety and mental stimulation. You might have multiple sources of income and may pursue different careers over your lifetime. Others see you as clever and resourceful in your work.

Your way of communicating with people helps you easily gain career opportunities through your charm. Networking and interacting with others are crucial to your success, and your reputation is often built on your ideas and how effectively you express them. You are respected and admired for your ability to multitask, manage your time well, and then switch flawlessly into conversation.

Having **Venus** in the **Tenth House** brings a charming and skillful energy to your professional relationships. You might meet your partner at work, or they could be a business partner, and you're inherently drawn to authority figures, and you may even embody that authority yourself. Your future spouse might come from a well-off background or be successful in their own right, possibly showing some Capricorn qualities. Your partnerships can really boost your career, whether through collaborations or the support of a special someone.

Sometimes, your partner might be older and share your hardworking attitude. In your career and public life, you're often well-liked and tend to succeed because you come across as balanced, graceful, polite, sociable, and genuinely passionate about what you do. Your career choices might lean toward areas associated with Venus, such as art, law, beauty, fashion, interior design, entertainment (for example, modeling, acting, or singing), floristry, weddings, finance, or any field that values aesthetics and social elegance. Your kind heart, charisma, natural beauty, and the way you make others feel special all boost your confidence.

While you enjoy feeling appreciated, it's well-earned because you also dedicate yourself to making others feel good. You work hard and deserve the rewards that come with it. Your attractive nature naturally draws people in, and your beauty is a wonderful asset.

Mars in the **Tenth House** brings out your competitive and ambitious side, placing it front and center in your public life and career. You are the kind of person who pursues your goals relentlessly, regardless of the obstacles, and you care deeply about your reputation. To the public, you are a bold individual who can lead. Your assertive leadership style suggests a potential future in politics, business, sports, athletics, dance, military, personal training, or an active lifestyle.

You tend to dislike authority and may resist being told what to do by those who use their position to intimidate others, especially you. This is because you have a natural inner authority that projects outwardly as a strong leader. You are the type of person who wants to climb the professional ladder rather than stay stuck where you are. Once you achieve a goal, you set another one.

Although you inspire others with your energy, be mindful of conflicts and practice patience. Not everything needs to be a confrontation. You are a go-getter who likes to get things done. You wouldn't enjoy sitting and doing nothing for a career; you need to be out there making progress toward your goals. You know you can't do that from the couch. Your passionate energy might sometimes be mistaken for aggression, even if you're just expressing a different opinion. Be aware of this because it reflects the image you want to project.

When **Jupiter** finds its place in your **Tenth House**, you naturally enjoy good fortune in your career and how others see you. Success seems to flow to you effortlessly. This expansive planet, when teamed up with the house that features your public image, opens up exciting opportunities and helps you build valuable connections that can even boost your career early on. People tend to recognize and admire your work, seeing you as wise, inspiring, and eager to share your perspectives.

You're often seen as a trendsetter, with a style that others love to emulate. Your passion for helping charities and your dedication as a humanitarian make you well-known in your community. The more you acknowledge this generous energy and give back, the more positive rewards come your way. Others are drawn to the optimistic vibe you radiate, making you a magnet for new ideas, inspiring new partnerships, and exciting opportunities that can lead to greater achievements.

Your reputation is quite strong, and the way you present yourself can influence this for better or worse. Your career might involve fields like education, social media, consulting, government, law, publishing, travel, writing, photography, philanthropy, or spirituality. You could find yourself working in a different culture or country than the one you were born in. Ultimately, your public image often reflects your honesty and enthusiasm for growth, making you a truly inspiring presence.

Do you have your **Saturn** in the **Tenth House?** If so, your professional life and public image are shaped through hard work, discipline, patience, and lessons learned over time. You may not be a natural hard worker, but you develop perseverance as you face setbacks and delays, with your efforts eventually paying off. Recognition might come slower than for others, but your dedication ensures lasting success.

Motivated by a desire to build a meaningful legacy, you take your obligations seriously and value being appreciated for your expertise. Authority figures, such as a strict father or mentor, may have set high standards that fuel your ambitions. You may become well-known for your achievements, especially in leadership, management, or roles that require long-term vision and responsibility. Fields such as law, politics, business administration, real estate, engineering, government service, or other careers that require strategy and discipline are suitable paths for you. As your experience grows, you may find fulfillment in public service, teaching, or mentoring, with your most significant achievements often emerging in later life, making your legacy memorable.

If your **Uranus** is in the **Tenth House**, your career path may be eccentric and unpredictable. You likely won't follow a traditional career route. It's clear that you tend not to conform to societal expectations, and this is reflected visibly in your life. You feel driven to contribute something meaningful and original to society because of your innovative ideas and charitable nature.

Uranus brings uniqueness and instability to your occupational choices. You are a thinker, opinionated, and sometimes this might rub others the wrong way if they don't understand your perspective. You might pursue unconventional work or take on unusual jobs most people wouldn't dare try. You could switch jobs suddenly, especially if they don't align with your values, or you might even create an entirely new approach in your field.

Activism, technology, science, innovation, media, communication, humanitarian work, and community projects can shape how you're perceived, both publicly and professionally. People see you as unique and ahead of your time. Your career may involve breaking harmful traditions, challenging authority figures, or introducing groundbreaking ideas to the public. Just be who you are, no matter what others think.

Neptune in the **Tenth House** shows that you are incredibly creative in your career, and your public image might sometimes seem a bit idealized. People often see you as inspiring, mysterious, or even captivating. You are alluring to others; they want to get to know you, but sometimes find it hard to truly understand you. To be honest, though, you get a lot of unwanted attention, which might sometimes feel overwhelming or make you wish to step back, especially if you're being recognized for things you're not entirely proud of.

Neptune here links your career to imagination, spirituality, or compassion. You might find yourself in fields like medicine, healing, therapy, art, music, film, fashion, poetry, writing, spirituality, or charity work. Figuring out the perfect career path may take some time, especially if you're unsure about your professional direction. Clarifying your goals and setting healthy boundaries can help you make better decisions along the way.

Sometimes you experience dips in motivation, and you might struggle to find your ambition. During these times, it's common to feel confused about your true calling, sometimes turning to substances or to fantasy rather than taking practical steps toward your goals. It's okay to feel lost at times, but remember, finding your career will come. It can take time to find your purpose, but when you do, your inspiration will flourish. You're meant to use your compassion and vision to create positive change in the world.

When **Pluto** is in the **Tenth House**, you have a passionate drive to achieve your goals and a desire to make a meaningful impact in your public life. You likely value respect and carry a strong, commanding presence. This placement can help you grow through your public efforts and become quite influential.

Although you do remarkable work driven by your intensity, you might encounter a boss who is domineering or overbearing. You may even experience some betrayal in your career from a coworker, if not your boss. This loss and betrayal could even be publicly visible.

Your career might undergo major changes early on. You may be very creative in what you're envisioning, but over time you could shift into something entirely different from what you initially imagined. This journey might include endings that lead to more powerful beginnings. You may be attracted to positions of authority, leadership, research, interrogation, law, investigation, finance, therapy, crisis intervention, spiritual work, working with the occult, social work, emergency response, hospice care, caretaking, taxidermy, or even roles such as a funeral director or mortician. Essentially, anything involving change, research, and the cycles of life and death, whatever allows you to influence other people and create an insightful difference.

Others might see you as authoritative, compelling, or intimidating in your career. If you have this placement, you could face public challenges that test your spirit, but each time you rebuild, you emerge stronger and more significant. You come into your power when you find a career that aligns with your truth and helps you connect with what truly resonates with your soul.

11th House: The House of Friendships & Aspirations

Ruler: Aquarius
Fourth Quadrant (Houses 10–12): Public Image & Life Path

The 11th House is all about friendships, social groups, charities, activism, and community influences. It encourages you to network and find supportive people who understand your dreams for the future. This house is a space where you can set your intentions, dream big, and think about how community support can help you achieve your goals. It also relates to humanitarian causes, technology, and social progress. You might find yourself reflecting on ways to give back and the causes that truly resonate with you. What do you hope to contribute, and what kind of future do you imagine having?

The 11th House is all about connection and community. It shows how your goals go beyond just yourself, emphasizing the importance of building friendships, joining clubs, or participating in larger societal movements. This house helps you find your place within social crowds, feel a sense of belonging with friends, and become comfortable with group dynamics. The zodiac sign on the cusp influences how you present yourself publicly, engage with others inside of your community, and can even point to inspiring mentors who offered support and guided you on your journey.

For example, if you're an **Aries Rising**, your 11th house is likely in Aquarius, which naturally rules this house. Your friendships, alliances, and social connections are wonderful areas where you can truly excel. They're opportunities to be brave, approach things with independence, and share your originality and enthusiasm. You're often drawn to groups that challenge the status quo and embrace revolution or envision a better future for all.

You have a talent for inspiring others to think outside the box and approach problems in fresh, innovative ways. Your long-term dreams tend to be bold, forward-thinking, and often at the cutting edge, reflecting your willingness to take risks for causes you believe in and ideas you hold dear. You value friends who respect your uniqueness and your need for independence. You thrive in communities that encourage creativity, individuality, and teamwork.

Sometimes, you play a special role in social causes or in how others connect and make friends, often supporting those who feel overlooked or misunderstood by society. This placement can also indicate friendships with people who are younger than you, not always, but many with this cusp have someone in their circle who is younger or perhaps has a younger spirit. Even you may be the younger-spirited one. You might connect with people who push you to grow and see the world through a different perspective, sometimes in surprising, delightful ways. Occasionally, you attract friends who challenge your boundaries or test your patience, but these experiences usually help you better understand who you want to build friendships with in the future. Overall, your social circle is a special space where your imagination, energy, and guidance naturally flow. Your ability to connect with forward-thinking, open-minded people can leave a positive, lasting impact on your life and the communities that you cherish.

If you're an **Aquarius Rising**, your Eleventh House is ruled by Sagittarius, which means you tend to approach friendships and social circles with a sense of adventure and seek out open-minded friends. You're likely to find it easier to connect with fun, happy, outgoing, philosophical people. You like to connect with others who want to grow in life, explore the world, discover other cultures, and enjoy learning new things, just like you.

You can easily make friends and have a lively social circle, which is terrific! You love to socialize. Just remember to take some time for yourself so you don't get overwhelmed or burnt out. It's all about finding that good balance.

You thrive in groups where everyone shares a common goal and often take on leadership roles to organize collective efforts. Your kindness, honesty, and enthusiasm inspire those around you, creating a warm and motivating atmosphere. You genuinely enjoy connecting with friends from different backgrounds, building meaningful relationships that could lead to exciting opportunities, whether it's through community projects, personal goals, or dreams you are passionate about.

When the **Sun** shines in your **Eleventh House**, you naturally brighten up in your community and bring warmth to those around you. People truly value your presence and look up to your inspiring nature. Your influence often stems from your rare causes, encouraging others to follow your lead because your actions are so distinct. Many are attracted to your originality and feel inspired to express their own uniqueness just like you do.

You genuinely enjoy spending time with friends, connecting with like-minded groups, and being part of communities that resonate with your ideas. These connections can open new doors, helping you move closer to your dreams and supporting your goals along the way. With the Sun here, your sense of who you are is deeply connected to your friendships and social circles, giving you a vibrant, Aquarius-like energy. You cherish your independence, even as you love working with others.

Sometimes, you step into a leadership role, and other times, you prefer to handle things on your own terms and do it your own way, with no rules you have to abide by. Your passion for technology and creativity excels through in your interactions with your community and friends, especially when you combine the two. Your love for community and making new friends stems from your innate humanitarian spirit, and your dislike for injustice comes from a deep desire for fairness and equality for those who need it most. You thrive hardcore when collaborating within a team or working toward shared goals, and you might feel called to social change or humanitarian efforts.

You can see what needs fixing in the world and stand up for what's right. Your inner light often highlights truths others might overlook, inspiring awareness and positive change. In astrology, the Sun also symbolizes a father figure. Your father may have shared some Aquarian traits. Intelligent, witty, friendly, yet possibly emotionally distant or reserved.

Having the Moon in the **Eleventh House** means your friendships and sense of community profoundly influence your emotions. You're naturally open-minded, warm, and friendly, making it easy to get along with others. However, you're also quite selective about who you let into your inner circle. You prefer genuine, meaningful connections over superficial ones.

Despite appearing outgoing, you value deeper bonds because your past experiences have made you cautious. With close friends, you often take on a caring, "Mom" role, checking in and offering support. Your friends tend to confide in you, knowing you're a loyal and dependable presence who always has their back. Your feelings about friendships may change over time, reflecting your dynamic nature.

You enjoy socializing across multiple groups, making you a true social butterfly. When you're among friends who share your ideals, you feel most fulfilled. This placement emphasizes the importance of expressing your individuality and being accepted for who you are. Independence and freedom are essential for your emotional well-being, though you might sometimes seem distant, shaped by your past experiences.

Since the Moon is connected to the mother in astrology, you might have felt her as emotionally distant at times or more like a friend, which helped foster your independence. Ultimately, you find great happiness in supporting causes you care about and forming meaningful bonds within your community.

Having your **Mercury** in the **Eleventh House** shows that you're passionate about making positive changes in the world, something that I really admire. Your unconventional thinking pushes you beyond societal norms in your community and among your friends, making your perspective truly unique. With Mercury, the planet of communication, residing in the house of dreams and aspirations, your voice is powerful and commands attention. Don't hesitate to speak your desires into existence and believe in them as if they are already yours.

People with this placement have a wonderful gift for manifesting through words, often becoming brilliant, engaging conversationalists. Your compassionate nature drives you to stand up for those who can't, and your innovative ideas have a magnetic charm. You likely have a wide range of knowledge and enjoy some lively discussions, especially when exchanging ideas with your friends. Keep in mind that sometimes others might see you as a know-it-all, but that's just because you're sharing your honest thoughts.

You love being around smart and interesting people, and although you're selective, your social circle can be pretty diverse. Engaging in group chats and witty banter energizes you, and exploring different viewpoints expands your understanding of the world. Whether through social media, writing, or speaking, you enjoy sharing your vision with others publicly. Your friends look to you for advice, and you're consistently encouraging them to dream big and chase their goals.

If your **Venus** is in the **Eleventh House**, love might be closer than you think, maybe right under your nose! You may not even realize it, or perhaps you do? Having this Venus in your chart often means that your heart could find its match through friendships or within your social circles. You might meet your special someone through a friend or even via social media, depending on your situation.

Whatever the case may be, it's essential to take your time and really get to know each other. This helps reduce any pressure sometimes associated with new romantic interests. There's no need for rigidity or urgency; love here flourishes when it's natural and patient. In time, it will come to you.

This placement also makes you a great candidate for a social media influencer! You have a magnetic vibe and are truly fascinating. People love watching you because there's something uniquely beautiful and alluring about you, whether on TV, your phone, or any other device. You can use this gift to your advantage, and some do by raising awareness for causes that matter, standing up against injustices, and making a real difference with your guidance.

You're attracted to people who share your dreams and moral values. You get along easily with almost everyone because your natural vibe is so welcoming and positive. But it's important to recognize the difference between simply getting along with someone and being best friends on a soul level, not just being an acquaintance. Venus here is about independence and personal space. Your loved ones sometimes don't understand that you cherish your time with friends and love your friends to the point they are like your own chosen family, your sisters or brothers, not someone you don't spend time with. The connection is much closer.

Suppose your **Mars** is in the **Eleventh House**. In that case, you direct your energy toward achieving your goals, trying new things, and taking on leadership roles, especially in group settings, due to your visionary outlook and big dreams. You're passionate about social causes and often motivate others to think innovatively, but your assertiveness may sometimes create friction with your friends. Mars here makes you ambitious and competitive, always striving to make your mark and push boundaries. Independence is imperative to you, and resistance to authority can cause conflicts when the ego intervenes.

You focus on collaboration and building networks, thriving as a project initiator. You're drawn to intellectually challenging friends who share your vision and are inspired by your determination. However, impatience in social situations can lead to misunderstandings. Your assertive enthusiasm for causes is contagious, ensuring you are heard. As a natural problem solver, you think creatively to overcome obstacles and inspire others. Balancing your drive with diplomacy will strengthen your friendships and reduce conflicts later on.

Jupiter in the **Eleventh House** brings warmth and support through friendships and communities that help you succeed. You might find yourself taking on a role as a religious or spiritual leader within your circles. In certain challenging placements, there could be a tendency towards cult-like behaviors, but this isn't true for everyone, and some may not be religious at all. Regardless, your beliefs have a meaningful impact on those around you.

You might be a beloved guru, teacher, or guide within your friend group or community, and sometimes, a friend might play that inspiring role for you. Your personal philosophies and worldview often influence how others perceive you, and you're usually surrounded by caring, supportive people. You are ambitious and your dreams go far beyond the scope of what others might think is possible, imitating your incredible spirit and outlook on life.

You often find yourself surrounded by friends who inspire you to grow, support your pursuit of goals, or open new doors for you through their connections. These friends can help you discover a job, introduce you to your partner, or play a key role in your journey to fame. When you're with the right people and energy, it's as if opportunities start to unfold naturally, almost like the universe is rooting for you. Networking becomes especially meaningful for you because you tend to meet the right people at just the right time.

Occasionally, so many opportunities through friends and social groups can make the choice overwhelming. You should be mindful of overpromising or taking on too many projects at once. Your optimism inspires others, and many of your friends see you as a motivator or someone who lifts their spirits. You have a gift for encouraging others to dream bigger, reminding them of what's possible if they just believe.

You have big dreams of making the world a better place. You imagine projects that help not just you but everyone around you. Humanitarian efforts, social movements, and initiatives that do good often attract you like a magnet. You might find yourself traveling to support your local community, engage in charity work, or connect through a network that spans the world.

If **Saturn** is in your **Eleventh House**, your friendships and goals may take time to develop and might come with responsibilities. You might sometimes feel isolated or as if you don't quite fit in with your community, but this is Saturn teaching you're the art of patience and how to be selective, reminding you that not everyone will be your friend or has your best interest at heart. As you mature, you learn the value of quality over quantity, and the friendships you build tend to be long-lasting, loyal, and dependable. Your social circles may start small, but they are meaningful, and you may be around people much older than you or in groups with significant age gaps.

You could feel responsible in groups, often becoming the one that others count on or who sets the rules. There can be a sense of restriction, like your goals and dreams take longer to come true, but Saturn rewards your perseverance, and when you stay consistent, what you create in this house lasts a lifetime. Sometimes Saturn here can make you feel like an outsider, but it also pushes you to find your true tribe and those who support your long-term visions. Your friendships may involve tough lessons or karmic ties, and you may need to let go of people who no longer support your path.

Over time, you might find yourself taking on management roles or becoming a figure others turn to for wisdom, thanks to the maturity you've developed through your social experiences. You may have learned the importance of hard work, but you may also feel that friendships and social freedom need to be earned rather than freely given.

Having **Uranus** in the **Eleventh House** suggests that your friendships are wonderfully unique and often have a delightful, quirky twist. You're organically drawn to an eclectic mix of people who are fascinating, eccentric, or simply unconventional by today's standards. This means you might find yourself magnetically attracting friends from all sorts of backgrounds, cultures, or lifestyles that are a little outside the norm, inspiring your view of the world. Unexpected changes in your social circles can bring new opportunities and even influence your life's direction. Your community connections tend to be lively and full of surprises, offering fresh perspectives that can significantly shift how you see things.

You're likely to gravitate toward friends who share your passion for progressive ideas and innovative thinking, whether it's about social reform or the latest technology. Friendships can sometimes happen quickly or end just as swiftly, which might feel overwhelming at times. Yet, each experience helps you grow, encouraging you to embrace change and develop a new skill set in adaptability and finding your place. You probably feel most alive when you connect with groups that challenge the usual way of thinking, and you're excited to discuss unique causes with your friends.

Feel free to explore some new ways to connect and work together, as your friends can be inspiring pioneers ahead of their time, sparking your creativity with their inventiveness and boundary-breaking spirit. You often imagine a unique future and aspire for your contributions to stand out and make a meaningful impact. Technology, social media, and innovative ideas can be tools to bring your dreams to life. Your community and friends are usually there to cheer you on and support your ambitions.

Having **Neptune** in the **Eleventh House** adds a magical, creative, and sometimes dreamy touch to your friendships and social life. You might find that your social circles feel enchanting and inspiring, though at times, navigating your place inside a friend group can seem a bit confusing. It's natural to feel like an outsider until you find some like-minded souls who truly understand you. Your optimistic view of people is a beautiful trait, but remember to stay on high alert, so you're not taken advantage of.

Setting firm, clear boundaries can help you. Sometimes, friendships may seem destined to last forever. However, Neptune's influence can lend a bit of vagueness, leading you to romanticize your connections and risking possible disappointment if reality doesn't match your hopes. You're drawn to making friends with people who inspire your creativity, spirituality, and vision for a kinder world, and you feel pulled toward spiritual or community healing efforts. This placement often enhances your social life with a spiritual, artistic, or humanitarian touch.

You may feel pulled toward artistic or charitable groups where empathy, intuition, and idealism are the topics. Your distracted energy influences your long-term dreams. You have imaginative goals that extend beyond the material or conventional realm, often envisioning a more beautiful, compassionate, and united world, with spiritual guides helping you along the way. You genuinely enjoy helping others, especially those with inspiring stories like yours.

Pluto in the **Eleventh House** intensifies the dynamics of your friendships, making them deeply transformative for you and often karmic. You are selective and cautious in group settings, guarding yourself as only a few truly know you. Temporary feelings of isolation signal a change toward having more meaningful relationships. You trust your instincts about people and keep your distance from those who make you uncomfortable.

Power struggles and boundary tests shape how you approach friendships. Your community ties are rarely superficial; they carry destiny and depth. You draw friends and mentors who challenge you and open up opportunities. You may advocate for change, lead others quietly, or expose issues that some had no clue about because of your passionate vision for meaningful change. Over time, the collective change imitates your personal evolution, empowering you to form lasting, authentic bonds with those who are worthy.

12th House: The House of the Subconscious & Secrets

Ruler: Pisces
Fourth Quadrant (Houses 10–12): Public Image & Life Path

The 12th House is the most mystical and spiritual part of your chart, full of secrets and hidden characteristics. It influences your subconscious mind, your dreams, and your intuition, guiding you through unseen worlds and personal mysteries. This house also represents endings, closure, and surrender, helping you release what no longer serves you. Here, you connect with feelings and truths that are hard to put into words but can be felt down into your soul. It's a space where healing, instinct, past lives, karma, and the collective unconscious come together. Exploring this part of your chart encourages you to look inward and discover the areas of yourself that exist beyond the physical world.

This house invites you to take gentle moments for yourself to relax, retreat, or simply rest away from everyday chaos. It's a warm space for solitude, helping you to recharge spiritually and connect with your higher self and spirit guides. You might notice old patterns or self-sabotaging behaviors that keep you stuck until you become more aware of them. At the same time, this house is a gateway for celestial guidance and inspiration, fostering spiritual breakthroughs. It's a safe haven to connect with something greater than yourself, whether you call it God, the Universe, or the collective. What matters most is the connection. Additionally, this house can uncover hidden wounds and experiences, as well as your gifts and talents. The sign on the cusp offers insight into how you approach healing, endings, and the unseen parts of your life.

If you are a **Cancer Rising**, then your Twelfth House falls in Gemini. This could mean your internal world is curious, talkative, and mentally active, but on a more private level. You are a reserved person and prefer to keep to yourself. You process your emotions and feelings through intuitive patterns such as studying, learning, writing, or reflecting inward, often discovering multiple perspectives on experiences. Journaling, teaching, learning, speaking, talking, and using your mind can be healing for you.

As a child, you may have tried to speak your truth and might have felt punished for being honest and expressing yourself. This can affect how you communicate with others as you grow older, sometimes making you question if you are smart enough to speak up because, in the past, you may have felt foolish for using your voice. It may seem difficult to relate to your people and others because of a deep-rooted fear of vulnerability, but you actually want to connect and open up. You just feel uncomfortable doing so, even though you daydream about being vulnerable.

Mysteries, secrets, hidden beliefs, and unintentional influences can all play a role in shaping your decisions. It's common to find yourself deep in thought, sometimes overanalyzing. Be mindful of gossipers and people who enjoy discussing others' affairs, as they might misinterpret or distort your words. Embracing spiritual growth and shadow work is fueled by a genuine curiosity and a heartfelt desire to explore and connect ideas.

Are you a **Libra Rising**? If so, your private world, with Virgo on the Twelfth House cusp, is shaped by self-reflection, attention to detail, and a desire to grow. This can sometimes lead to an inward perfectionism, where you thoughtfully analyze your thoughts and actions, occasionally being your own harshest critic. You find comfort in routines and structure to nurture emotional stability, yet you might feel the need to "fix" yourself before sharing your true self with others.

Beneath the surface, you yearn for forgiveness and inner peace, yet you might find it hard to let go of self-judgment and the fear of losing control. Your wish for harmony and the worry about being misunderstood often make you cautious about revealing your true self. Early experiences may have led you to link your self-worth with how productive you are, which can sometimes lead to self-doubt and exhaustion later in life. However, what you really desire is to treat yourself with kindness and gentle understanding.

Your healing journey is all about finding a gentle balance between caring for yourself and growing as a person. Remember, you don't have to earn love by being perfect. Ultimately, your spiritual growth means embracing your spirituality, establishing meaningful rituals of care, and discovering peace through acceptance and nurturing of yourself.

If you're a **Capricorn Rising**, having Sagittarius in your Twelfth House indicates that you have an expansive inner world. You are on a quest for understanding the purpose of what happens after life. You might often keep these feelings close to your heart or find it challenging to share them openly. Deep inside, there's an extreme longing to resolve the pain from past traumas and power struggles.

During peaceful, personal moments, you might notice your intuition becoming clearer and having vivid dreams that gently guide your subconscious healing process. Facing any repressed feelings or past desires can be very beneficial, and you might consider doing so through therapy. Ignoring these feelings could sometimes lead to compulsive control-seeking behaviors or even self-sabotage. You might notice recurring cycles of feeling isolated or wanting to be alone to recharge and understand who you are more deeply. Just know it is okay to take time alone, but utilizing this time to embrace your spirituality can really help, especially if you are feeling lost and unaware of what your purpose is. Journaling, learning, traveling, and meditation are some healing practices that can benefit you as well. Having a good self-care ritual would do wonders for you.

Growing up, you might have felt like you were the kid who experienced everything around you on a more poetic level. You are creative, spiritual, philosophical, and intuitive, and you love learning about other cultures and religions, but you didn't feel comfortable sharing those feelings or any information with others. You may have some karmic debts to pay from past-life occurrences or from being irresponsible in some way. You probably developed your psychic abilities early on, and you might have escaped into the other realm often or found yourself daydreaming and using your imagination frequently, specifically if the outside world was overwhelming for you. Be aware of escapism tendencies by avoiding reality through using substances to block out the past.

Do you have your **Sun** in the **Twelfth House**? If so, you may present yourself in a Piscean way that is compassionate, dreamy, empathetic, and mysterious, with a touch of gypsy energy that makes your presence both gentle and magnetic. You could be introverted and enjoy solitude, often excelling at emotionally supporting others and encouraging self-care, though you might struggle to offer the same help to yourself. This placement gives you a behind-the-scenes presence that requires private time to recharge and reconnect with your spirit.

In solitude, your creativity, spiritual pursuits, and subconscious work really shine. However, you might still find yourself feeling uncertain about your identity and having a hard time fully understanding who you are. Growing up, you could have felt out of place or had your confidence shaken, making it challenging to express your creative side and sometimes leaving you feeling unseen or like an outsider. This feeling of being disconnected might lead to struggles with escapism, addiction, or experiences with institutions, where regaining your sense of power becomes so important. But even with these hurdles, many people with this placement don't realize just how brilliant and mystical their quiet light truly is, as it silently influences others far beyond the physical realm.

You aren't boastful; many find you admirable and feel spiritually supported by your deep connections. You're often guided by ancestors and spiritual guides who brighten your way and help clarify your purpose.

Dreams can be a special window for insights and intuitive messages, so keeping a journal might be a fantastic way to remember and reflect on the wisdom you receive while you sleep. Your philosophical insights, strong intuition, and natural link to the unseen or collective unconscious truly make you a talented guide, healer, or spiritual teacher in emotional and mental areas.

In astrology, the Sun is often seen as a symbol of the father or a father figure. When it appears in the Twelfth House, it can represent emotional distance, absence, or challenges. These experiences can guide you to find strength and a true sense of identity from within. Over time, you come to realize that your quiet light holds a powerful healing energy, capable of comforting both yourself and others.

Having your **Moon** in the **Twelfth House** means your emotions are extremely personal, and you tend to keep your feelings private. You have a natural sensitivity, empathy, and intuition, often picking up on the energies around you, which makes spending time alone very important for your recharge. Remember to carve out quiet moments for your spirituality and well-being. Dreams, meditation, journaling, or creative pursuits can be incredibly healing for you because your subconscious often sends you important messages through them.

You've likely learned to manage your feelings independently, gaining strength through self-reliance, even if it sometimes feels lonely. Since the Moon influences your instincts and emotional security, its placement here makes you highly aware of hidden emotions, your own and others', drawing you toward healing and helping others on a deep, spiritual level. Just keep in mind that your own care is essential. This position enhances your spiritual sensitivity, allowing you sense things before they happen and feel the collective energy of the world around you.

Be cautious of using distractions or habits to escape from true feelings, as you tend to explore your subconscious and seek guidance from higher spiritual sources. This heightened sensitivity can sometimes feel overwhelming, so taking time for periods of withdrawal can be a sacred space for renewal and internal wisdom. In astrology, the Moon can also symbolize the mother, and you might have experienced complex or distant maternal relationships. Maybe she wasn't around much, or perhaps if she was, she was significantly in touch with her creative and spiritual side. Was she a struggling addict or a tortured soul? Or did she have a deep connection to the other side?

Mercury is in your **Twelfth House**, which means your thoughts and communication are often private and often hidden, making it hard to express exactly what's going on inside your mind. You might feel like your brain is quietly working in the background, gathering information, processing it, and observing everything closely, but you're not always ready to share what you've learned. This might make you seem quiet or reserved, but it's not that you have nothing to say; you simply prefer to think things through on a deeper level before speaking. You're incredibly intuitive, often sensing the moods, feelings, and unspoken thoughts of others, and your insights can sometimes seem almost psychic.

This placement offers you a gift for understanding dreams, symbolism, and the deeper layers of life. Engaging in activities like writing, journaling, poetry, or creative pursuits such as singing or acting can do wonders for you by providing a meaningful way to understand your inner world. Your mind works in creative and abstract ways, often receiving sudden insights or intuitive flashes that support your spiritual growth, research, or practices that look beneath the surface. Sometimes, you might worry about saying the wrong thing or not being fully understood, which can make you hold back your words and experience self-doubt. Remember, your unique perspective is valuable, and sharing your thoughts can help you connect more deeply with others.

Your childhood experiences, like being told to stay quiet unnecessarily or dealing with minor speech delays, may have influenced how you communicate today. These moments often teach you patience, sharpen your listening skills, and help you appreciate the importance of using your voice. Mercury in the Twelfth also connects your mind to the collective unconscious, allowing you to pick up on unusual patterns, premonitions, or visions from beyond what we physically see. You might feel a natural urge to speak up for those who don't have a voice or to share truths that others tend to overlook or try to ignore. Embracing solitude is essential; during quiet moments, you can process your thoughts, recharge, and turn your reflections into some of your greatest strengths.

When **Venus** resides in your **Twelfth House**, you are a spiritual healer. Your loving nature, sense of beauty, and the way you relate to others tend to be gentle, private, and deeply spiritual, often kept close to your heart. Those with this placement might not always see their own beauty, but their personal depth naturally draws others in. You could notice feelings of jealousy in relationships or sometimes feel as if others are against you.

For those with Pisces or Twelfth House placements, setting clear boundaries is especially important. You often cherish keeping your affection private or feel drawn to hidden, secretive relationships, valuing privacy as a form of protection. This might create a longing for elusive love, as if you're searching for a special soulmate elsewhere. Your experience of love is often mystical and romanticized, and you are inclined toward self-sacrifice or loving those who are emotionally unavailable.

You're likely to gravitate toward creative, spiritual, or struggling individuals and tend to avoid those who resist change. Your Venus gifts you with strong intuition and empathy in matters of love, but be mindful of taking on others' burdens too much. Keep an eye on over-giving, as it can attract emotional vampires; those who drain your energy. Venus also lends a dreamy, ethereal quality to your art, music, or writing, often inspired by moments of solitude.

Growing up, you may have learned to love quietly because of absent, uninvolved, or troubled parents, which may lead to a sense of caution and privacy in adult relationships. But as you grow, you'll start to see your sensitivity as one of your greatest strengths. Your journey is leading you toward a mature, deep love that honors both your empathy and your need for boundaries.

Having **Mars** in your **Twelfth House**, your drive and ambition work quietly behind the scenes, subtly shaping your actions. Your emotions, especially anger or frustration, are often internalized because early lessons taught you to hide your feelings or avoid conflict. This is not a weakness; it reflects a learned coping mechanism. Suppressed emotions can accumulate and erupt unexpectedly, particularly when a loved one is threatened.

As a result, you are motivated to protect the unseen or overlooked, yet you prefer to avoid the spotlight. The Twelfth House links your energy and ambitions to old emotional patterns and childhood conditioning, including challenges with self-assertion. To navigate these challenges, channeling this energy into spiritual healing or creative outlets helps with your emotional transformation, primarily through meditation, journaling, yoga, solitude, or home workouts.

Early experiences may have created inner frustration or confusion about sexuality, influencing how you express yourself. Additionally, exposure to conflict can make you hesitant to assert your needs, causing bottled-up emotions or passive responses. Physical activity and creative expression help release tension and process feelings. Despite these struggles, you possess quiet resilience and offer support from behind the scenes. A central life lesson is in learning how to express your emotions honestly and set healthy boundaries while channeling your drive into protection and healing.

If your **Jupiter** placement lands in the **Twelfth House**, you will find that you are very lucky, and blessings often show up in mysterious, hidden, or silent ways. Jupiter here watches over you, protecting you from behind the scenes, like a guide working overtime when you don't even realize it. You may feel that someone or something always saves you at the last second, preventing situations from getting worse. It's possible you have survived accidents or near-death experiences that most wouldn't have, because unseen forces protected you.

This position often creates a profound relationship with mysticism, faith, and the spiritual world, as Jupiter expands your subconscious mind. Growing up, you may have felt the need to keep your dreams, beliefs, or creativity to yourself, as there wasn't always a safe space to share them. For some, your good fortune may not have fully appeared until later in life, once you have embraced your spiritual side.

Because the Twelfth House can involve hidden enemies, Jupiter here may bring challenges with being too generous or trusting, so setting boundaries is essential. This placement can also carry a tendency to escape through addictive behaviors, making healthy coping essential. You are deeply empathetic and can naturally put yourself in someone else's shoes. Spiritually, you are drawn to mysteries, meditation, healing, and hidden wisdom, and your intuition and psychic abilities are strong. When you surrender rather than try to control your blessings logically, Jupiter works everything out for you sometimes through your dreams, quiet visions, or sudden, unexpected strokes of luck.

If responsible **Saturn** is placed in your **Twelfth House**, you may possess a quiet inner strength that few people notice. Much of your personal growth occurs in solitude, allowing you to process fears, insecurities, and restrictions internalized from any early experiences. Authority figures may have been strict, distant, absent, or emotionally unavailable, shaping your sense of structure and boundaries. The Twelfth House adds mystery and reflection, often making self-discipline and limits self-imposed or repressed.

You might feel a tension between wanting control and recognizing your true limits, especially during times of stress or isolation. In your youth, asking for help may have been discouraged, forcing you to develop independence early. You likely give generously but may not receive equal support back, bearing burdens and expectations alone without assistance. This can lead to high personal standards, self-judgment, and quiet fears of failure, rejection, or punishment.

However, this placement also encourages growth in discipline and structure in a unique and mature way. Over time, you'll find yourself gaining inner wisdom and strength, helping you to handle internal struggles more effectively. As you progress through life, you'll often support others quietly, offering guidance from behind the scenes. Practices like healing, solitude, and shadow work, such as journaling, meditation, therapy, or exploring spirituality, in processing fears, reset boundaries, and cultivate patience, along with embracing your natural pace.

When **Uranus** is in your **Twelfth House**, a sense of rebellious energy quietly dwells within your subconscious. This planet of freedom sparks unexpected visions, strange dreams, and personal spiritual awakenings that you tend to keep to yourself. You might feel like an outsider or a black sheep, sometimes unsure how to share your unique qualities with others.

As a child, you might have felt different without knowing exactly why. To others, you might have seemed complicated or difficult to understand, so you only shared your ideas when you felt truly safe. Keeping your true self hidden helps you look "normal," but inside, your imagination yearns for freedom. This can create an internal tug-of-war between fitting in and expressing your true individuality.

You might find yourself overwhelmed by psychic flashes, sudden insights, and prophetic dreams, especially when you're young and still learning to understand these experiences. Childhood moments like unexpected disruptions, changing family situations, or emotionally distant parents may have made you more sensitive to chaos and unpredictability. Some people with this placement might struggle with self-sabotage or sudden disturbances, even while chasing their goals. However, Uranus in the Twelfth also brings a deep desire for freedom paired with a need for stability and consistency. Your unique perceptions and intuition can be truly inspiring but remember that embracing your individuality and expressing it entirely is the key to fulfillment.

When **Neptune** is positioned in the **Twelfth House**, you tend to feel things very deeply. You often pick up on the moods and energies of those around you without even realizing it. Unlike in other areas of your chart, Neptune's energy flows softly here, as it feels very much at home. This placement inherently nurtures your compassion, empathy, and selflessness.

However, it's important to remember that this compassionate nature can sometimes lead you to become a bit too absorbed in your idealistic views about people. You often have a calm desire to help those who are suffering, even if your efforts go unnoticed or unappreciated. This caring nature can sometimes border on self-neglect if you don't set healthy boundaries. Reflecting on your childhood, you might have been very sensitive, easily overwhelmed by noisy environments, or deeply absorbed in others' emotions, which could have sometimes left you feeling drained.

Remember, it's essential to find time for retreat and self-care, as you naturally act like a sponge, soaking up everyone's struggles. You're into spirituality, mysticism, and creative pursuits like meditation, prayer, music, painting, or writing, which bring you peace. Your dreams often feel very real, filled with symbolism or even prophetic glimpses that offer you understanding of what is to come. Dreams can serve as a way to connect with loved ones who are on the other side.

Sometimes, the line between reality and imagination blurs, especially in youth, leading to feelings of confusion or escapism, or making you feel misunderstood. Learning to manage this sensitive nature is a lifelong journey, and finding healthy ways to process your emotions helps prevent your feelings from becoming overwhelming. Over time, these moments of retreat evolve into a source of inner strength, giving you profound emotional wisdom, empathy, spiritual insight, and a powerful intuitive sense.

Having **Pluto** in your **Twelfth House** means you experience life intensely beneath what others can see. You tend to keep strong emotions private, often dealing with feelings like anger, fear, or powerlessness on your own. In your early years, you might have learned to hide these intense feelings, sometimes even self-sabotaging or suppressing parts of yourself because they seemed like they were "too much" for others to handle. This placement supports a rich inner world full of self-reflection, growth, and deep psychological insights.

You have a wonderful gift for healing old wounds and helping others through trauma or cycles of control and power. Many people with this placement find themselves drawn to psychology, spirituality, or even intense religious paths. Childhood experiences might have left you feeling powerless, extremely cautious, and highly sensitive to mysterious tensions or emotional issues. Exposure to family trauma or abuse could have helped you develop resilience, intuition, independence, and survival skills early on.

Learning to confront and understand these hidden energies is a lifelong journey that involves solitude, reflection, and shadow work. Embracing these lessons allows you to heal, transform, and come out of life's challenges stronger. Spiritual awakenings along your path deepen your self-awareness and understanding. As you grow older, you tend to move through the world quietly, often observing, learning, and turning your experiences into inner strength and wisdom.

House Systems

Let's chat a bit about house systems in astrology! If you're just starting on your quest for learning astrology, it might seem a bit overwhelming at first, or at least it was for me, but I can promise you, it's actually simpler than it looks. Think of a house system as a way to break down your chart into twelve different parts, each representing a different area of your life. For example, one house might be about your career, another about your relationships, or even your early home life. It also covers personal growth, finances, and friendships, you name it! The way these houses are divided can influence how you interpret a chart, so it's helpful to explore your options and find what works best for you.

When I first started learning astrology on a deeper level, once I got over just knowing my sun sign, I realized how much more complex it is. However, **Whole Sign Houses** quickly became my favorite method. It's probably the simplest way to understand houses, especially when you're just starting out. The concept is straightforward: each zodiac sign corresponds to one house. For example, if your Ascendant or Rising Sign is in Leo, then Leo is your first house. Virgo becomes your second, Libra your third, and so on, wrapping all the way around the chart. One sign equals one house. I really love this approach because it makes it so easy to see which sign influences different parts of your life without overthinking or complicating things.

But here's the other thing: I also use **Placidus**, and many other astrologers do as well. Unlike whole sign, Placidus works a bit differently. It calculates house sizes based on your exact birth time and location, so some houses may be larger or smaller, which can change where planets fall and shift your chart's perspective. Many people appreciate Placidus because it offers a more detailed view of timing and life patterns. It might seem a little confusing at first, but don't worry, you will get it soon!

There are many house systems out there, like Koch, Regiomontanus, and a few others. However, as you're just starting, you don't need to learn all of them right away. It's a good idea to focus on one of the most popular systems initially as you explore and learn. The great news is that there isn't a strict right or wrong choice. It really depends on what helps you read your chart clearly and what you feel most connected to.

My personal tip is to start with the house system that feels right for you. For me, that was Whole Sign because it just made sense and was easy to learn. I also did some research and found that many people find it the easiest way to get started. Once you feel comfortable, you can explore other systems, such as Placidus, and see how their interpretations might be different. Some people even combine them, like I do, using Whole Sign for a broad overview and Placidus for timing or a deeper understanding.

Think of astrology as a helpful guide rather than strict rules. Its purpose is to make your path more transparent and more understandable, not to cause confusion. So don't stress, just find the system that resonates with you, try things out, and trust your instincts. You've got this!

Degrees & Aspects

Now, let's talk about degrees and aspects, because this is where astrology really becomes detailed. Up until now, we've discussed planets, signs, and houses, which give you the big picture of your chart. But degrees and aspects? They add the specifics, that little fine print, and this is the information that makes your chart unique to you. Degree theory can even help you predict major life events.

So, what do degrees in your birth chart mean? Degrees mark the exact position of a planet in the zodiac wheel, and each one has its own significance. Every planet in your chart isn't just in a sign; it's at a specific degree within that sign. Think of it like giving directions. Saying "I live in Sagittarius" is broad, and the person might get lost, but saying "I live at 5° Sagittarius" is precise, avoiding any confusion. That degree matters more than you might think because it changes how your planet expresses itself. Some degrees are especially powerful. Such as:

Critical Degrees (0°, 29°): These are the most significant degrees in astrology.

0° is powerful and represents fresh, new, raw beginnings, bringing in the pure energy of that sign. This embodies the zodiac sign wherever you see this degree in your chart.

29° This is an arenitic degree, which signifies the final phase of that sign before it transitions into a new one. It is also known as the "Fame Degree." For example, if you have a 29° Leo Sun, it indicates you have mastered all the lessons associated with being a Leo. Wherever this degree appears in your chart, you might feel a push to grow.

But critical degrees aren't the only ones you should be aware of. Some astrologers also consider other special degrees that can appear in your chart and add more flavor to how a planet expresses itself. These include:

2° often carries early lessons, pushing you to act harder, explore new opportunities, or figure out your place in relationships and life early on.

17° is called the fated or karmic degree, and it indicates areas of life where events feel destined, lessons come in a way that's hard to ignore, or patterns repeat until you've learned what you're meant to.

28° often feels like the push to fully step into their power before moving into the next sign, like wrapping up lessons and preparing for the next chapter of growth. This degree represents success.

Degrees can make a significant difference; two people might both have Venus in Leo, but if one has it at 6° and the other at 29°, their ways of loving and showing affection will feel very different. That's why degrees can add depth to your chart that you wouldn't see if you only looked at planets in signs.

Here's where things get interesting: Degree Theory! Each degree in the zodiac reveals special hints about the timing of life's moments. For instance, 0° often symbolizes new beginnings or birth, while 2° might remind us of toddlerhood, when those early lessons are first learned. Around 17°, it could connect to the age of 17, a period when life begins to teach some important lessons. Degrees like 28° and 29°, which come towards the end of the cycle, carry a feeling of intensity and completion, possibly relating to ages 28 or 29. From there, the cycle naturally moves forward, guiding us through these meaningful stages.

If you're curious about something that happened at age 44, you'll want to look at around 14° in the next cycle. Once you know where your planets are sitting in your chart, the next step is to explore how they interact with each other. These interactions, called angles or relationships, show how your different energies come together, support one another, or face challenges. Here are the main ones you'll encounter:

Conjunction (0° to 5° apart)

This happens when two planets are in the same zodiac sign and are very close, within just 5 degrees. Their energies come together, blending and interacting like a single force. This can be a beautiful harmony or, at times, a challenging and intense one. For instance, a Sun + Mercury conjunction can beautifully boost someone's communication skills. On the other hand, if the planets are in conflict, like Mars + Saturn, it might cause some tension and feelings of restriction, making actions feel more difficult.

Sextile (60° apart)

This is an excellent and positive connection between placements that are 60 degrees apart, two zodiac signs away, and within 5 degrees of the start of that sign. Imagine it like two planets really enjoying each other's company during this time. They share a playful Venetian vibe. Sextiles offer opportunities, help shape your talents, and create a natural flow. However, you usually need to take the initiative to make the most of them. They won't do the work for you, but they'll open doors if you're willing to step through them on your own. Here, the planets support each other by providing helpful services to one another.

Square (90° apart)

Squares can be pretty challenging, much like two planets that don't quite see eye-to-eye and are constantly fighting with each other. The planets are usually "squaring up" (see what I did there?) and occur when planets are 90 degrees apart and three signs away within the same modality. While they push us out of our comfort zones, they also encourage us to grow by helping us work through obstacles.

Trine (120° apart)

Trines are wonderful blessings and are considered very positive angles in the chart. When planets are positioned 120 degrees apart within the same element, it creates a sense of harmony and natural talent that flows effortlessly. The planets involved seem to understand each other beautifully, and their energy connects smoothly. A little tip? Sometimes, trines can make you feel a bit relaxed or lazy because they don't require much effort from you.

Opposition (180° apart)

Oppositions are similar to two kids fighting over the same cookie. Two planets that are 180 degrees apart are pulling the energy in opposite directions, making you feel the need to find a balance between them. This can feel like a constant push-and-pull, but it also teaches you to combine opposing energies and find a compromise.

So, when you look at your chart, think of degrees as coordinates that show exactly where your planets are, and aspects as the relationships between those planets. They reveal how planets are working together or against each other. Without them, you'd just have a list of planets floating around randomly, but with them, you get the full story of your challenges, gifts, and opportunities for growth.

The beauty of astrology is that it doesn't just show your strengths but also points out where you might face challenges. It's often those tougher aspects in your chart, like squares or oppositions, that help shape the incredible person you're meant to become. On the other hand, the easier aspects like trines and sextiles serve as gentle reminders of where things can flow smoothly, helping you feel more in sync with your journey instead of constantly fighting against an uphill battle.

Understanding Your Career and Money in Houses: 2, 6, & 10

When thinking about your career, finances, and your life's calling, it's helpful to focus on three key areas: the 2nd, 6th, and 10th houses. I like to call these the "Money Houses" because they reveal how you earn money, how you serve others, and how you present yourself in the world. Paying attention to these can provide valuable insights into your path and purpose.

The **2nd House** is all about your money, abundance, resources, possessions, and what you truly value. It reveals how you earn a living and your relationship with money itself. Do you feel safe and secure when you have money? Or do you find it hard to hold onto it? Do you see money as a source of comfort and stability, or does it tend to slip away easily? The second house can also offer clues on how to increase your earnings. One helpful step is to look at your 2nd house in your birth chart and see which zodiac sign rules that house.

To discover the best ways for you to make the most money in your lifetime, begin by exploring your 2nd House. First, identify which zodiac sign governs that house. Next, find the planet that rules that sign. Then, look for that planet in your chart and see which house it resides in. This house will show you the area of your life where money and abundance can most likely come your way, opening doors to new opportunities.

If you're a **Virgo Rising**, then **Libra** rules your **2nd House**. Since Venus rules Libra, your next step is to look for Venus in your chart. For example, if Venus is in your **10th** House, then your money could come from areas like public speaking, working in the same field as a parent, or even starting your own business and being your own boss. This suggests that your financial success is connected to the reputation you build and the legacy you leave behind.

Here's a helpful example: if you are a **Cancer Rising**, then **Leo** rules your **2nd House**. Leo, being ruled by the Sun, means you can find the Sun in your chart. If your Sun is in the **12th House**, it suggests you might find opportunities to earn money through spiritual pursuits, behind-the-scenes work, or roles within institutions. It also points to using your creativity in solitude and being an artist, helping others express their feelings, or using your unique gifts to make a difference.

I want to share that the **2nd House** represents how you earn money, and the **8th House**, directly opposite it, shows how you might receive money through others' resources. This could include shared finances, investments, inheritances, taxes, or even your partner's income. While it's not exactly about earning money on your own, it describes ways money can come into your life through partnerships. I bring this up because the 2nd and 8th Houses are like two sides of the same coin: what is yours and what comes from others. Seeing both perspectives helps you get a clearer picture of how money can flow into or out of your life.

The **6th House** represents your daily routines, work habits, and the small but important ways you care for yourself and others. It's where your habits reside and how you organize your day, your attitude toward helping others, and how you manage your responsibilities, from work to caring for pets. Think of it as the area that reflects your regular, day-to-day life rather than your long-term legacy. Do you enjoy having a structured day, or do you find it difficult?

For example, if you're an **Aquarius Rising**, your **6th House** is ruled by **Cancer**. This shows that your daily work and routines often involve caring for others, offering comfort, and forming emotional connections. You might find joy in jobs that nurture people, in working from home, in running a home-based business, or in creating a family-like atmosphere at work. Your life could focus on building security and caring for your health with compassion or serving others in a way that feels protective and supportive.

The **10th House**, also known as the *Midheaven*, is the highest point on your birth chart. It represents your public self, your career, reputation, and what you're known for in the world. Think of it as the area where you leave your mark and build your legacy. This placement can offer insights into the kind of professional path that might bring you success and a clearer sense of your life's purpose. It's more than just your job; it's about the role you play in society and what others admire about you. The 10th House helps answer the big questions: "How will others remember me?"

If you're a **Sagittarius Rising** and **Virgo** rules your **10th House**, it can give you a reputation for being organized, detail-oriented, and somewhat of a perfectionist. You communicate thoughtfully and analytically. People with Virgo in the 10th House often excel in careers that demand precision and problem-solving, such as editing, research, healthcare, or any role where technique and planning are key. Since Mercury governs Virgo, its placement in your chart adds even more distinction.

For example, Mercury in the 9th House might connect your career and public image to teaching, publishing, traveling, or spirituality. You may feel inspired to motivate others with your knowledge, help expand their perspectives, or guide them through personal growth. Your legacy could involve leaving others better equipped to think critically and approach life with clarity, all while embodying the practical diligence that Virgo naturally demonstrates.

Remember, your career and your purpose don't always have to be the same. Sometimes, your job helps you pay the bills (2nd House), your daily routine keeps you grounded (6th House), and your true calling reveals itself in another way (10th House). There may be times when all three perfectly align, and you feel completely in harmony. Neither way is wrong; it simply depends on your chart and what's in tune with your soul's journey.

Exploring Your Partnerships & Relationships in the 7th House

The 7th House governs your close relationships, such as romantic partners, business partners, and even notable rivals or secret enemies. It shows the qualities you're drawn to in others and the kinds of commitments you step into. It even exposes the lessons you gain through these meaningful connections.

To better appreciate and understand your relationships on a more personal level, start by looking at the sign on your 7th House cusp and see if there are any planets nearby. This can give you insights into the kind of partner you might attract and the overall energy of your relationships. To get an idea of where and how you might meet your special someone, find the ruler of your 7th House, the planet that governs the sign on your 7th cusp, and see where it is in your chart. This shows the area of life where your relationship is most likely to begin.

For example, if you are a **Taurus Rising**, **Libra** influences your **7th House**. Your partner might have a peaceful, balanced energy to them and be a very charming romantic. It's likely your relationship will be committed and more on a soul level. It will feel very fun, loving, and harmonious. You might meet your partner having fun, in a social setting, around art, or in a place of justice; you could even meet them in an environment that is associated with beauty. For more information, you look to **Venus,** she rules **Libra**. If **Libra** is in your **5th** House, you may meet them while out having fun, maybe at a party or a social event with friends. It's likely when you're feeling vibrant and playful with your inner child. You could meet during a creative moment, while spending time with friends, or even through mutual friends. Sometimes, relationships begin when you're exploring your hobbies and doing what truly makes you happy.

If you are a **Scorpio Rising**, **Taurus** rules your **7th House**. This suggests your partner is likely to be an exceptionally financially stable person who genuinely wants to care for you. They come across as very grounded, sensible, attractive, and supportive. Sometimes, they might struggle with feelings of jealousy in your relationship. Additionally, since **Venus** rules **Taurus**, if **Venus** is in your **4th** House, your partner could enter your life through a family connection or while you're at home. It might be someone who lives nearby, like a neighbor or a school classmate. You may have known them since childhood, and your bond could feel nurturing and stable. Overall, it seems your partnership will focus on creating a safe, secure space where you both feel truly supported and cared for.

If you're curious about when you might meet someone special or even tie the knot, it's a good idea to look at the movements of Venus and Jupiter. Venus, the planet of love, and Jupiter, the planet of luck, when they move through your 7th house, can bring exciting opportunities for new relationships or help deepen your current partnerships. Often, this can lead to important commitments, such as engagements or marriage. Venus tends to make love feel more effortless, sparks attraction, and enhances romance, while Jupiter can broaden your social circle, helping you find a partner who truly resonates with your path. Keeping an eye on these transits can give you a gentle nudge about the right timing, so you're more aware of when love or partnership might beautifully enter your life.

Final Thoughts

As you reach the end of this book, I hope you've come to see astrology through a fresh and inviting perspective. It's more than just a collection of signs and planets; it's an ancient, living language that speaks to your very essence. Learning astrology can be a bit tricky because it's both complex and straightforward, ancient yet timeless, practical yet poetic. It gently reminds us that we are here for a meaningful reason. Each of us carries a special map in our birth chart that shows our potential, highlights our challenges, and guides us on how to truly stand out in this world.

My journey with astrology has been truly enriching for nearly thirty years. One thing I've come to cherish is mastering this beautiful art. Every time you look at a chart, whether it's yours or someone else's, it reveals something new, another layer, a hidden detail. That's the magic of astrology; it grows with us and changes as we grow. What might seem mysterious today could make perfect sense years later as life helps us gather the experiences we need to understand it better. It's perfectly okay to explore and maybe get a little lost in those intriguing rabbit holes along the way! Whenever I notice something new in a chart that I hadn't seen before, it ignites my curiosity to explore how it might connect with other parts, making the whole puzzle even more exciting with each new piece I find.

I encourage you, no, I implore you to keep exploring your chart, look into others' charts, take notes, and learn as much as you can about how transits and cycles influence your life. Think of astrology as a helpful tool and inspiring guide, rather than a limit. Always remember, you have free will. The stars might set the stage, but you're the one who decides how to shine in the spotlight.

No matter if you pick up this book again next week or years from now, let it serve as a gentle reminder of how wonderfully complex you are, and that the universe truly flows through you. You are more than just your Sun sign; you're so much more than that. If nothing else, I hope this book offers you clarity and a sense of self-acceptance, helping you recognize your connection to something greater. May it also comfort you in knowing that you are part of something meaningful, and that your story is still being written.

Thank you so much for giving me the chance to share what truly brings joy to my story and my deep passion for astrology. I hope you keep gazing up at the sky each night with wonder and curiosity, knowing that the same stars that inspired ancient astrologers are shining down on you and guiding your path, too.

A.M. Douthit

Appendices:

Glossary of Astrology Terms

☉ Sun: This shining body symbolizes your core identity, vitality, and life energy, representing your main sense of self.

☽ Moon: In your chart, the Moon shows how you nurture others and respond with intuition and emotion, reflecting your inner world.

☿ Mercury: Mercury rules your communication, thinking, and learning styles, helping to understand your mental processes.

♀ Venus: Venus stands for love, attraction, beauty, values, and pleasure, emphasizing what brings happiness and harmony into your life.

♂ Mars: Mars indicates your drive, energy, ambition, and sexuality.

♃ Jupiter: Jupiter broadens your horizons with growth, wisdom, abundance, and many opportunities.

♄ Saturn: Saturn brings structure, discipline, responsibility, and important lessons.

♅ Uranus: Uranus ignites innovation, rebellion, sudden changes, and awakening.

♆ Neptune: Neptune is associated with dreams, intuition, illusions, spirituality, and compassion.

♇ Pluto: Pluto signifies transformation, power, rebirth, endings, and new beginnings.

Angle: One of the four main points of a chart: Ascendant, Descendant, Midheaven, and IC.

Ascendant (ASC / Rising Sign): The zodiac sign rising on the eastern horizon at birth; self-image and first impression.

Aspect: The angle formed between planets, indicating how energies interact.

Chart Ruler: The ruling planet of the Ascendant sign; influences personality strongly.

Composite Chart: A combined chart from two people's placements to study their relationship.

Conjunction (☌): An aspect of 0°; planets blend energies.

Cusp: The dividing line between two signs or houses.

Decan: A 10° subdivision within each zodiac sign, adding layers of meaning.

Degree Theory: The idea that each degree (1–29) holds unique symbolism.
Detriment: A placement where a planet is in the sign opposite its rulership; energy feels weakened or challenged.

Descendant (DSC): The point opposite the Ascendant; linked to relationships and partnerships.

Domicile: A planet in the sign it rules; feels most at home and strongest here.

Element: Fire, Earth, Air, Water; categories of zodiac energy.

Exaltation: A placement where a planet is particularly strong and dignified.

Fall: A placement where a planet feels weakened; the opposite of exaltation.

Grand Trine (△): An aspect pattern where three planets form a triangle of trines (120° each), symbolizing natural harmony and flow.

House: One of 12 sections of a chart, each representing a key area of life.

IC (Imum Coeli): The lowest point in the chart; it represents home, roots, and family.

Intercepted Sign: A zodiac sign fully contained within a house without touching any cusp; energy is harder to access.

MC (Midheaven): The highest point in the chart; symbolizes career, reputation, and public life.

Modality: Cardinal, Fixed, Mutable; describes a sign's style of expression.

Natal Chart (Birth Chart): A map of the sky at birth showing planetary positions.

Node (☊ North Node / ☋ South Node): Destiny points; the North Node indicates growth; the South Node signifies past patterns.

Opposition (☍): An aspect of 180°; indicates polarity, tension, and balance.

Orb: The number of degrees allowed for an aspect to be considered active.

Part of Fortune (⊗): A calculated point that indicates talents, prosperity, and natural ease.

Planetary Ruler: A planet that governs a specific sign (e.g., Mars rules Aries).

Progressions: A predictive method where the natal chart evolves symbolically over time.

Quincunx (Inconjunct, 150°): An aspect of awkward adjustment that requires integration.

Retrograde (℞): When a planet appears to move backward in the sky; associated with review and reflection.

Solar Return Chart: A chart created for the exact moment the Sun returns to its natal position; highlights yearly themes.

Square (□): A 90° aspect; represents challenge, tension, and growth.

Stellium: Three or more planets grouped within the same sign or house, indicating concentrated energy.

Synastry: Comparing two natal charts to analyze compatibility.

T-Square: A complex aspect pattern with two planets in opposition and both square a third.

Transit: The movement of planets in the sky and their influence on a natal chart.

Trine (△): A 120° aspect; signifies harmony, ease, and flow.

Yod (Finger of Fate): An aspect pattern where two planets form sextile and both quincunx a third; suggests karmic lessons or destiny.

Resources for Further Study

If you're curious about a more organized way to learn, I suggest checking out 'Astrology Made Easy' on Udemy, a course I created just for you. It's perfect for beginners who want to get familiar with the signs, planets, houses, and aspects. Plus, it'll equip you with the confidence to start reading charts on your own!

Books / Authors

For a deeper exploration, I love sharing some of my favorite astrology authors with you! Steven Forrest is a master of evolutionary astrology, offering philosophical insights into chart interpretation and personal growth that really resonate. Mari Silva makes astrology approachable and practical, making it easier for everyone to connect with. Additionally, authors like Liz Greene, Robert Hand, and Jessica Lanyadoo each bring their own unique perspectives on astrology, psychology, and spiritual growth, making your journey even richer.

Tools & References

Having an ephemeris nearby is a fantastic way to stay connected with planetary movements and better understand transit effects. It allows you to follow the planets with greater purpose and see how they gently influence your own chart over time.

Websites

I often suggest two websites: Café Astrology, known for its detailed chart interpretations, articles, and learning tools, and Astro-Seek, a handy resource for generating charts, tracking transits, and exploring progressions. These sites are great for anyone interested in astrology and eager to learn more.

Tip

Combining courses, books, and online tools gives you a well-rounded foundation in astrology. Begin with what feels approachable to you, and allow yourself to explore the deeper layers at your own pace.

Birth Chart Examples

All the celebrity birth data in this book comes from Astro-Seek, and I personally created the chart visuals. I chose to omit the lines to give you a clearer view of the charts and the planets' positions. Feel free to use these as helpful references as you explore different house placements and deepen your journey into astrology.

Lady Gaga's Birthchart

Sabrina Carpenter's Birthchart

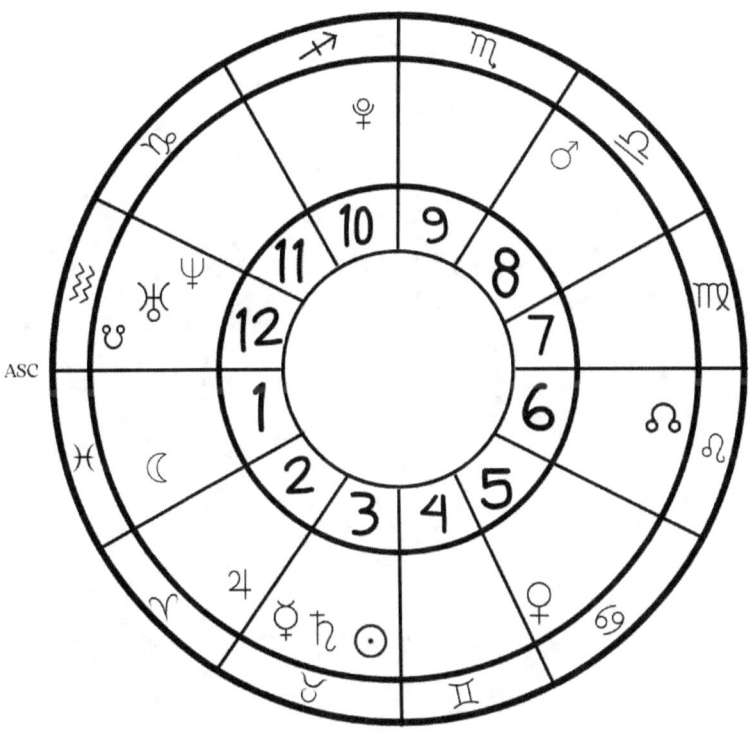

Kendrick Lamar's Birthchart

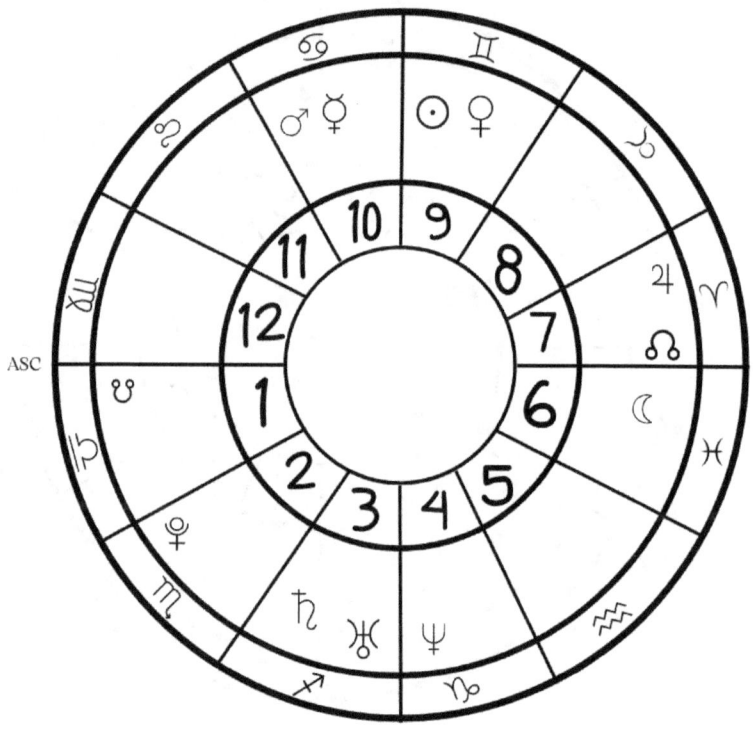

Robin Williams Birthchart

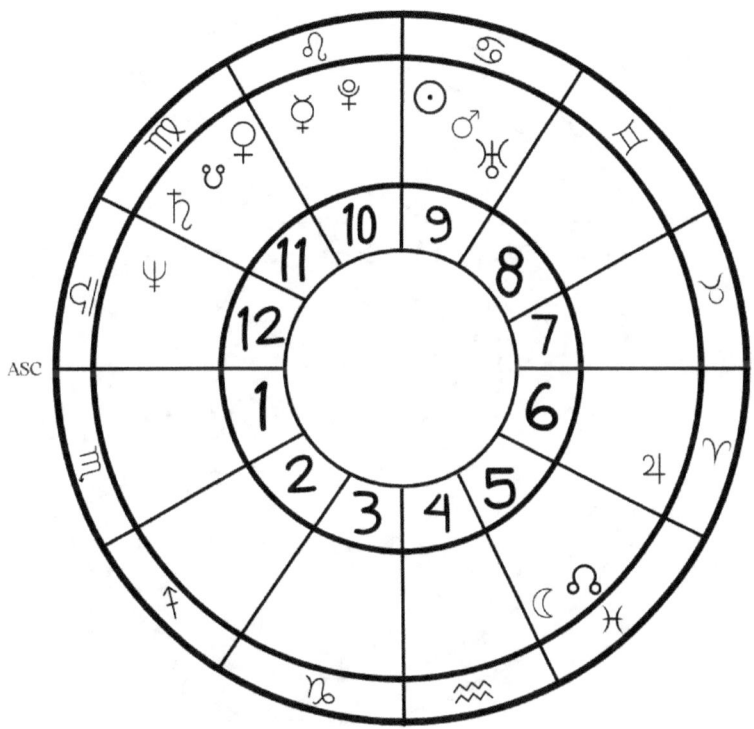

Madonna's Birthchart

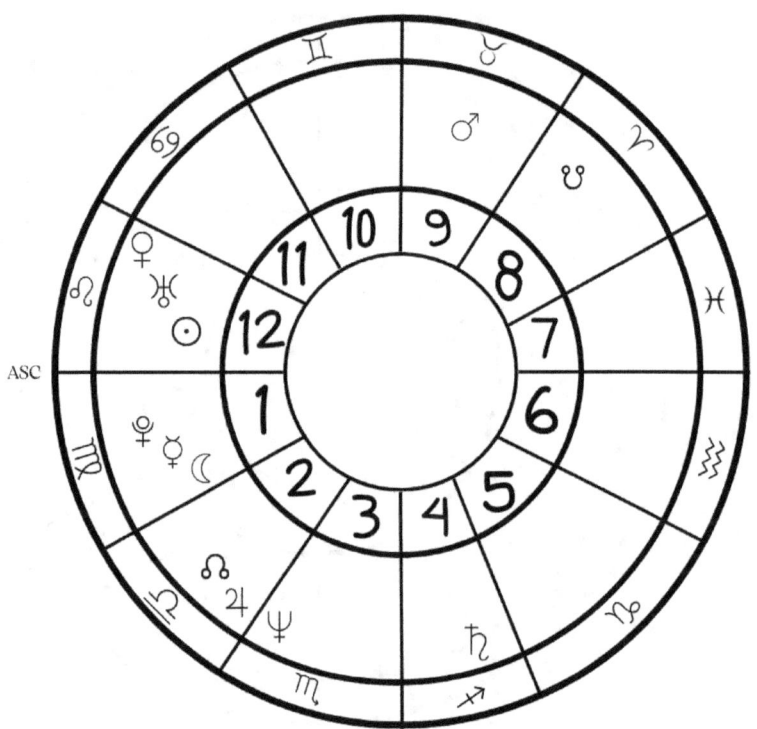

Shania Twain's Birthchart

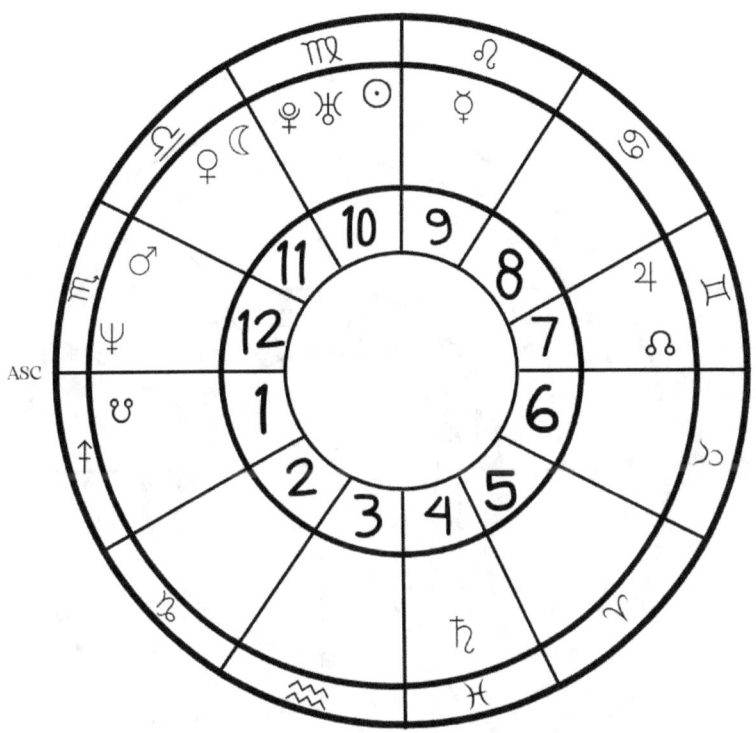

Snoop Dogg's Birthchart

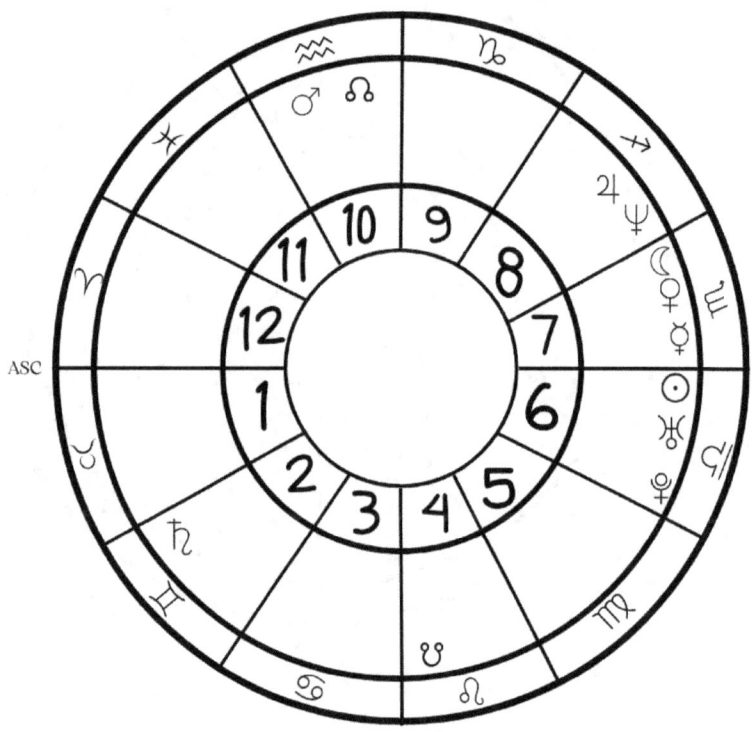

Pablo Picaso's Birthchart

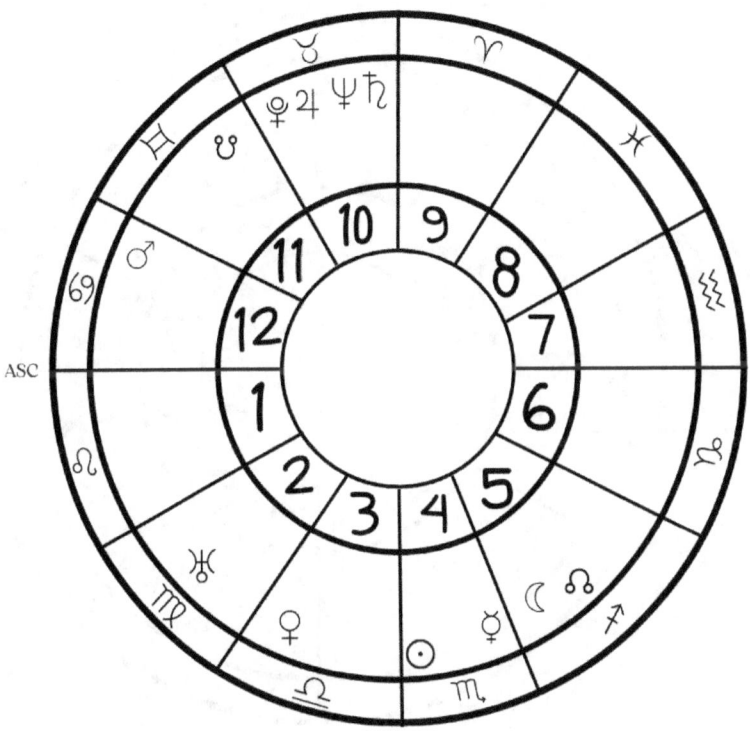

Taylor Swift's Birthchart

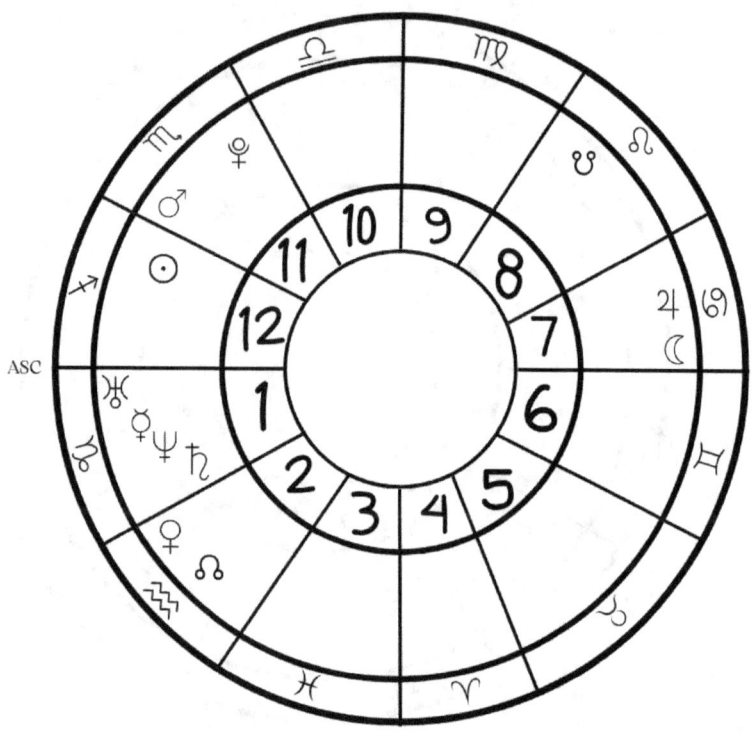

Rob Zombie's Birthchart

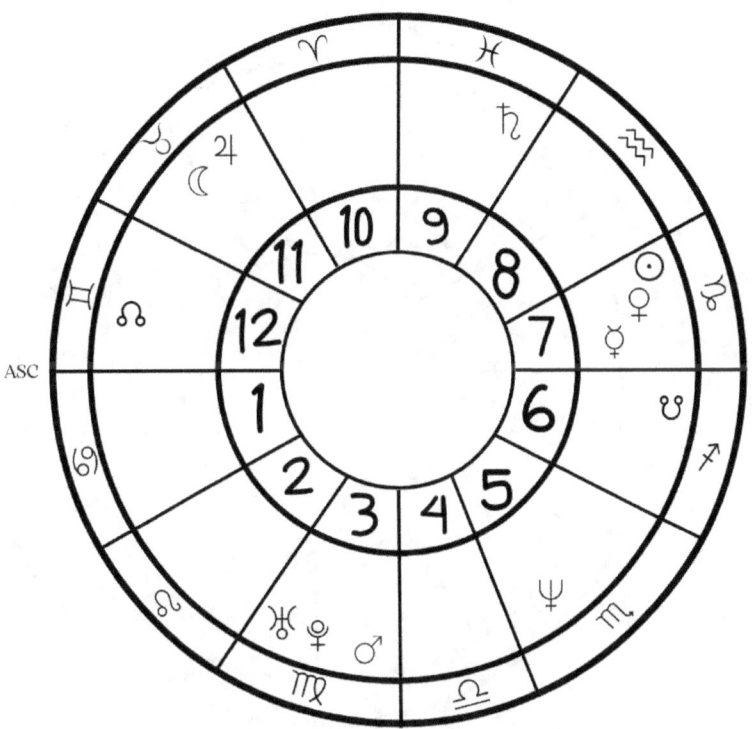

James Dean's Birthchart

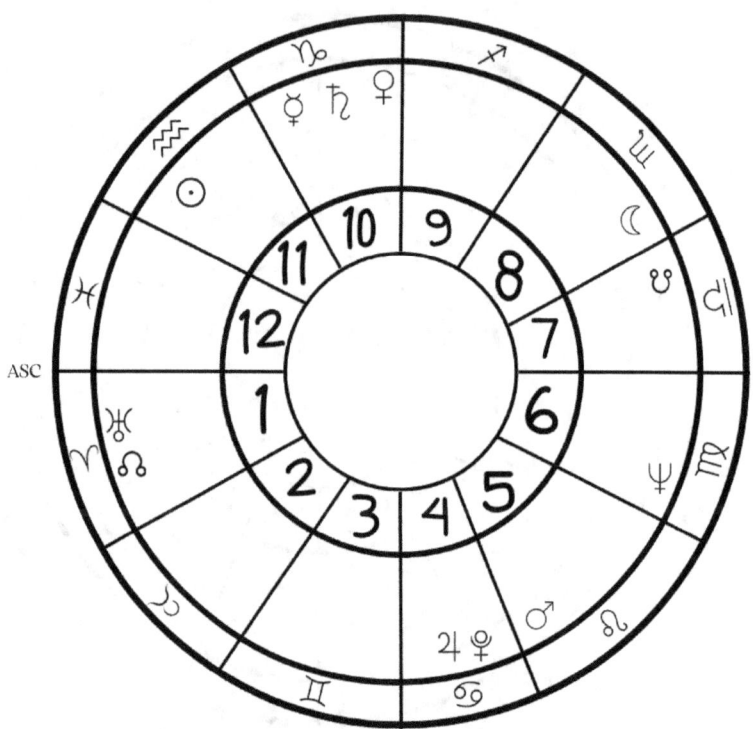

Chelsea Handler's Birthchart

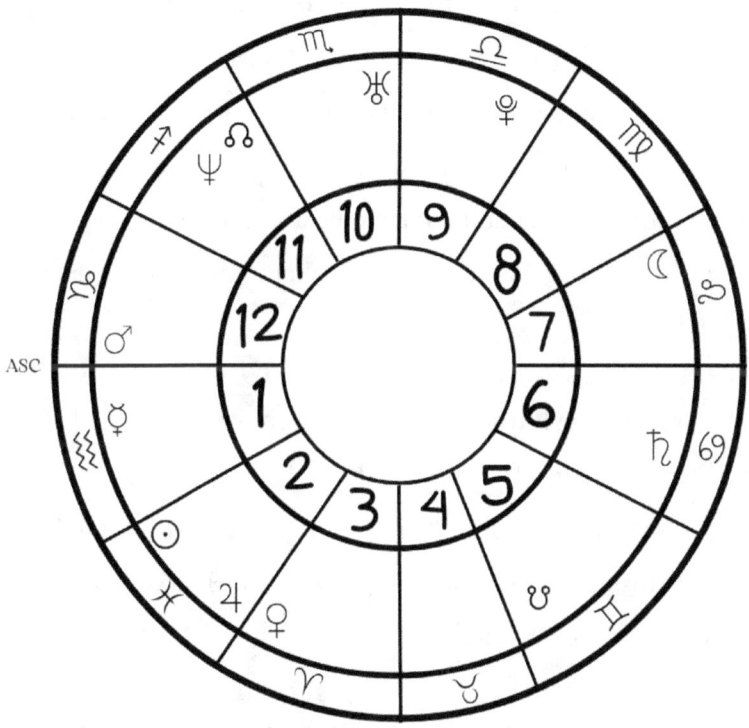

About the Author

A.M. Douthit (Ashley Douthit) is a passionate Teacher, Author, aspiring Therapist, and Spiritual Guide. With her Bachelor's Degree in Education and her current pursuit of a Master's in Counseling, she has inspiring goals beyond writing and teaching: to establish her own private practice as a Certified Therapist. This would be a cozy, welcoming space where others can feel authentically heard and start their healing journey. Ashley's heartfelt mission is to help others find their inner light amid the darkness.

She's a lifelong learner who sincerely enjoys exploring the mystical arts, including Astrology, Tarot, Palmistry, EFT, Metaphysics, Meditation, and energy work. Her passion for learning, combined with her talent for teaching, makes these spiritual practices feel accessible, exciting, and empowering for everyone.

Ashley, with a Virgo Rising, Leo Sun, and Sagittarius Moon, brings passion and heart to everything she creates. She shares her expertise through her Udemy courses, helping students expand their intuition, embrace their feminine energy, and walk confidently in their own truth.

She is also a devoted wife and mother of four who truly values spending quality time with her loved ones and friends. Outside of her work, Ashley enjoys simple pleasures like delicious food, meaningful tattoos, outdoor concerts, traveling adventures, playing with her dog, learning new things, and the joy of finding that perfect TV show to binge-watch. With her ever-curious spirit, she sees life as a continuous journey of knowledge and growth, always eager to discover new things that help her connect more deeply with herself and those around her.

Her mission is to inspire others to live unapologetically and celebrate their inner light. She encourages others to embrace the fullness of their feminine energy. She believes that life is full of everyday magic that's waiting to be noticed and cherished. Through her work, she gently reminds everyone to never give up on their dreams, no matter how distant they may feel, and to keep moving forward with courage and hope.

www.ingramcontent.com/pod-product-compliance
Lightning Source LLC
Chambersburg PA
CBHW060412130626
46555CB00005B/2037